Practical Course of Hypnosis
How to hypnotize, Anyone, Anytime, Anywhere

Special Workshop on modern hypnosis, trance and Hypnotic Phenomena, suggestions and inductions High Level Testing Suggestibility, Covert Testing, Convencers and Downriggers United hypnotics, allowing you master this wonderful masterful art of hypnosis *on a fantastic journey of training and practical learning,* **with the most advanced modern methodologies, the most effective techniques and strategies I finally let you take this skill to the next level.**

<u>Practice in this Course of Hypnosis in its special edition will learn to:</u>

- **BioReprogramar** you conscious and subconscious mind through modern methods and the most effective techniques of modern hypnosis.
- Suggestive master inductions as well as the most effective suggestions that allow you to strengthen your ability to generate trances and hypnotic phenomena high level in your coaching sessions, sessions clinical hypnosis, hypnotherapy, hypnosis show street and hypnosis show.
- Knowing the mental and psychological processes between mind (neuro), language (Linguistics), and the interaction between them (Programming), which will enable the correct use of hypnosis and persuasion with the tools of Applied NLP and Mental reengineering to reinforce your learning and training.
- Having a clear plan of action and well-defined step by step, allowing you to develop hypnotic and persuasive necessary to achieve new states of hypnotic trance "{(mental, emotional and psychological)}" skills.
- Increase Circle of Power and your level of strength or authority level to a higher level (FP) that allow you to develop your skills and create hypnotic orders, inductions and suggestions more effectively.

3rd Special Edition, *Revised, Updated and Extended (it includes exercises and Plan of Action) This book is an adaptation of the Transcription Course Online, Original audio and video*

Transformational Coach
Ylich Tarazona
Writer and lecturer International

YES, you can learn to hypnotize, anyone, anytime and anywhere. The issue is not, if you go into hypnosis, the question is, when you enter. Since everyone is hypnotizable if you know the "how" and "what" answers.

3rd Special Edition *Revised and updated by: Ylich Tarazona November 2017.*
Cover Design and development by: Ylich Tarazona
SEAL*: **Independently Published** © /Kindle eBook* **ASIN: B076G97F14**

ISBN-13: 978-1979723954

ISBN-10: 1979723958

BISAC: Hypnotism / Hypnosis / Self Hypnosis / Hypnotherapy / Hypnosis
YLICH TARAZONA the right to be identified as the author of this work has been affirmed by SafeCreative.org, Registration Code: 1710134545955 accordance with the Copyright Worldwide. **Publication Date***: November 18, 2017.*

COPYRIGHT

This book in its special edition called "HYPNOSIS COURSE PRACTICE -*How to hypnotize, anyone, Anytime, Anywhere* ©-® ". Adapted to learning **Modern hypnosis**, *Trance and Hypnotic Phenomena, suggestions and inductions High Level Covert Tests, suggestibility and Downriggers Convencers United hypnotics.* It is the intellectual property of YLICH TARAZONA © & Reengineering WITH MENTAL PNL ®.

FOLLOW THROUGH OUR OFFICIAL WEBSITE
http://www.reingenieriamentalconpnl.com

Legal assistance:
LAWYER: Mariam Charytin Murillo Velazco
CI: V-17502580, - INPREABOGADO: No. 158611

MENTAL reengineering NLP It is a virtual community for entrepreneurs. One of the Internet Website dedicated to providing COACHING in consolidating Skills and Development of Human Potential Maximum. Specialists in training, education and training of high level through NLP or Neuro Linguistic Programming, specializing in the supply of training and courses to achieve goals, objectives and consolidate effective Flesh results optimal performance; through a series of books, EBook's, Audios, Podcasters, Tele-Seminars Online, Audio-Visual Workshops, Webinars and Conferences Master of attending classes.

You cannot pretend to be associated with YLICH TARAZONA & MENTAL reengineering PNL in any form or use our name in connection with your own personal or professional practice, unless you are properly trained and certified validates that it proves that formally trained, properly trained or trained with us.

3rd Special Edition Revised and updated by: Ylich Tarazona November 2017.
Cover Design and development by: Ylich Tarazona
SEAL: Independently Published © /Kindle eBook **ASIN: B076G97F14**

ISBN-13: 978-1979723954

ISBN-10: 1979723958

BISAC: Hypnotism / Hypnosis / Self Hypnosis / Hypnotherapy / Hypnosis
Registration code: 1710134545955 / License: All Rights Reserved © by SafeCreative.org / Intellectual Property Registration Date: 18-Nov-2017.

CONTRIBUTORS:
Mariam Charytin Murillo Velazco
Ylich Leavitt Gabriel Peña Smith Tarazona
Jeffry Samuel Peña Tarazona
Genesis Zarahemla Odaylich Tarazona Maldonado

If this course of HYPNOSIS practice in its special edition has been interested and want us to keep you informed of our upcoming publications, editions, mini courses, special reports, video conferences, webinars, online and offline seminars, audio books, podcasters or our online services and offline as sessions, coaching, therapies, corporate events, courses, workshops, seminars, conferences and other activities classroom or instructional materials designed and created by the author & MENTAL reengineering PNL; write to us, telling us what topics are of interest and we will gladly keep you updated.

You can also contact the author directly via e-mail by:
MásterCoach.YlichTarazona@gmail.com

DEDICATION

- 5 -

Dedicated especially for you "APPRENTICE"

The content of this present book "HYPNOSIS COURSE PRACTICE - *How to hypnotize, anyone, Anytime, Anywhere ©-® "*. We provide the tools you require to start developing these hypnotic skills in the process of creating, styling and build your own Hypnotic Induction System Persuasive.

And this is my intention for you ...

Your friend **Coach Ylich Tarazona**

INTRODUCTION

Relevant information for this edition.

Hello such, my dear readers. First of all, thanks for purchasing this extraordinary book Hypnosis and hypnotism, I wrote thinking of you.

Before we begin, I want to communicate some essential changes I have made in this 3rd Special Edition. If you have some of my previous versions; You will see that I have made some revisions and important updates in the latest editions, as I seemed necessary to achieve fulfill the purpose for which I wrote this book for you. Among the changes I have made, I have incorporated a number of examples and practical exercises related to the lesson of some of the most relevant chapters. In the few cases where edit the text or change some content, they have been to adapt better examples and exercises recently incorporated in the present work.

These changes are almost imperceptible in most cases, since first of all I wanted to respect the original manuscript and the main idea of this book with its flaws and virtues. So, in the few occasions when I have incorporated some ideas, I've added some extra point or I added some elements of interest to my readers and learners, it is because I found convenient or necessary and vital to the proper application the principles of "***Modern hypnosis**, Trance and Hypnotic Phenomena, suggestions and inductions High Level Testing Suggestibility, Covert Testing, Convencers and Downriggers United hypnotics*" contained in this special edition.

> *If you had the opportunity to read some of my other printed or digital books, you have seen that both the literary style of my writing; and typographic characteristic style that I use when translating my ideas, seek a single purpose. Help you develop your full human potential to the next level, and allow a better understanding of the concepts, definitions and action plan that I share with all of you in order to help them internalize these vital and essential principles to your own life.*

To achieve this goal; at the end of some key chapters, I share a range of exercises that allow you to implement the essence of what you just studied. Likewise, I also offer them a series of summations or to reflect basic principles that will help you reinforce what you've learned.

Thus, champions and champions at the end of the book you will have real strategies, techniques, tools and effective methodologies that have been studied and tested over the years by the greatest experts in the field. Likewise, these principles have been implemented and put into action again and again by the same author, both as in their sections, shows and both virtual lectures and face personal level, with thousands of people who have applied these principles effectively to their own lives.

Such procedures have been routinely incorporated into this ADVANCED COURSE to guarantee optimal results by MODELS effective NLP or NLP APPLIED hypnosis and persuasion that have been checked through the years by the most renowned experts. Thus, avoiding the use of guesswork or simple theories.

For this reason, apprentice and dear readers, I'll give you some advice: Connect with the essence of this book, ACTIVELY LEE, every word, every line, every paragraph, every page, every chapter, every idea, every teaching, every example, every story, every exercise, every principle that love with all of you, and see how; gradually, step by step, line by line and precept upon precepts begin to have the excellent results required in each and every one of the most important and essential aspects of his life.

This course my dear readers is a powerful theoretical and practical for those who want to learn to develop effective tool hypnotic qualities. Of course, this book is not the only way to learn hypnosis. However, if you follow the directions step by step I in this book, and have the right attitude and the confidence, determination and commitment can assure you apply these principles in anyone.

It is important to note at this point that hypnotic skills you'll learn in this course ADVANCED involve a lot of responsibility and professional ethics. Always keep in mind that the correct application of hypnosis can be properly used, either for fun healthily and produce some laughter in our environment at some Hypnotic Show "or" we can also use hypnosis properly in therapeutic areas to generate large and extraordinary mental and emotional psychological changes in people in our coaching sessions or hypnotherapy. With this in mind, I want you to understand that this book gives you the information and resources needed in both cases to use hypnosis professionally and ethically especially so to ensure the welfare of all those involved in it. The use you give you will depend on your choice, but remember whatever purpose you want to achieve, you should always be based on the highest standards of professional ethics and decency, built on the principles and the highest moral values.

YOU IMAGINE all you can achieve getting to learn to apply these universal laws of success in your own life. You can imagine how your life would change dramatically for the better, to be able to conquer all fondest your dreams, goals and objectives you set out to achieve in this life, thanks to these basic principles to succeed. NOW POSSIBLE!

LITERARY AND MY STYLE WORKS TYPOGRAPHIC

The teachings containing my books and courses mostly, are a strategic combination mixed with powerful metaphors, parables, allegories, illustrations, stories, quotes and quotations that have been collecting and summarizing during the years from different sources; such as books and works of various authors (to which, granted them all the credit and recognition they deserve for their valuable contributions).

The objective of extracting extraordinary collection of these great and renowned writers and translate them into my works is; help them better understand my readers, I want to convey information subjectively. In this way; through learning of symbolic and figurative representations, you my friends to acquire the main ideas.

So; my books, through their quotes, famous quotes, thoughts, stories, reflections and illustrative narratives can become a source of inspiration to help those individuals with full purpose of heart they want to change and transform their lives continuously and permanently.

Another of the Typographical I use to write my work methodologies; It is to use different literary styles, introducing a variety of punctuation, bold, italic, underlined, letter case combinations, among other conscious repetitions of ideas and teachings transmitted several times; again, and again, but in different contexts and situations, to record them in your conscious and subconscious mind. As well as sometimes "strategically change the way you write and express my ideas intentionally first, second and third person" lie I transmit information, in order to make the most didactic, versatile and pleasant reading for all my readers.

Should this seem inappropriate or wrong at some point for some of my readers, I want anticipate them in advance that it is not in any way an oversight on my part, or lack of editing and transcription of the work. On the contrary, it has a clear objective and pursues a particular purpose. TRUST ME. It has a purpose for you, keep reading and you'll understand what I mean.

In another order of idea; Importantly also incorporated in the course of the book a wide variety of famous quotes, inspirational quotes scripture, Bible verses, philosophical concepts, examples, similes, exhibitions, descriptions and figured in the course of the whole work language. Since such expressions, concepts and ideas are able to subjectively stimulate a variety of sensations MULTI-SENSORY at both (visual, auditory and kinesthetic) that allow evoke images, sounds, sensations and emotions in the reader's mind.

Following the same order of idea; I include in all my works a series of positive statements, self-statements empowering, based on META-MODELS strategic NLP through a series of hypnotic commands and persuasive patterns that allow the reader to incorporate these suggestions and Subliminal inductions your mind conscious and subconscious, and producing them radically positive changes in their mental and psychological structure, creating in new neural connections more empowering.

And finally, APPRENTICE, among other resources I use are personal expressions like you and IT, to refer directly to my readers, with the sole intention that they can feel identified with my words, and have the full assurance and conviction that all I write my books thinking about them.

In the audible versions, such as in cases of audiobooks, podcasters, the Webminars, the Tele-Seminars and Online Conferences I use instrumental background music with sounds of nature, and at times binaural waves at different frequencies. To induce certain positive states in the brain. Among the many benefits offered by these powerful tools it is conducive to accelerated learning, conscious reflection, proper assimilation of ideas, mental alertness, stimulation of creativity, relaxation, concentration and meditation among many other advantages. As they have shown in numerous studies on the subject. Including the doctoral thesis Pedro, *which we report excellent and wonderful positive effects of these sounds, both psychological and physiological.*

The purpose of introducing this range of literary, typographic styles; METAPHORICAL and binaural (the latter only in cases Audible), merged with a varied set of techniques NLP or Neuro Linguistic Programming Applied Reengineering Principles Cerebral Neuro-Coaching autohypnosis among other tools. It is to enable my readers receive a transformational education more useful, holistic and comprehensive, enabling them to embrace new ideas, thus avoiding the slightest resistance to change, and creating a greater psychological impact - emotional in the retention process - learning.

******IMPORTANT******

This book in its special edition is a transcription adapted from Podcasters, Webminars, teleseminar, online course and face offline, Conference Coach Ylich Tarazona entitled "HYPNOSIS COURSE PRACTICE - *How to hypnotize, anyone, Anytime, Anywhere* © ® ". *For* that reason; this book reflects a unique and original style of transcription. Since it is an adaptation of a work Audio and Video Course Conference; rather than a literary work, written as such.

Table of Contents

- 15 -

CHAPTER FIRST: PRESENTATION AND GENERAL INFORMATION ABOUT HYPNOSIS

Hello such APPRENTICE, a big hello. I'm YLICH TARAZONA Transformational Coach, NLP Master, Specialist Mental bioprogramming, Reengineering Brain and Neuro Coaching. Ericksonian Hypnosis Practitioner, Hypnosis Psycholinguistics, Hypnosis and Conversational Hypnotist Show in Show. I hope you enjoyed my first book "**THE POWER OF HYPNOSIS** - **Theoretical and Practical Manual Training in Hypnosis and Hypnotic Persuasive Skills Development** ©-® Volume 1 ".

Where we learned the development of historical and evolutionary context of hypnosis through the ages ... we understood the multiple definitions, concepts and basic principle of ancient and modern hypnosis ... We also learned about the different theories, levels, degrees and states of hypnosis ... gave a brief overview of the reality and perjury behind the myths, legends and speculations about hypnosis ... study the differences and functions of the conscious mind, the critical factor, the subconscious mind and the unconscious of the human being ... among other interesting initial topics in our training as hypnotist, hypnotists, hypnotherapists or hypnotists ...

Now apprentice; I give this second part of the series: NLP Applied Influence, Persuasion, suggestion and hypnosis ... where I present this course of Hypnosis Practice © -® Volume 2 I have prepared, designed and created especially for you, hope you like it, enjoy it and especially you bring your hypnotic skills to the next level. So, without further ado let's begin.

The reason and purpose; by which I decided to get a 2 and 3 volume of my book in print, digital and online version. It is really poor practical information of interest and actual effectiveness of hypnosis can be found on the Internet, for that reason; I decided to create and summarize, therefore this course Hypnosis Practice for you my dear readers and learners. My aim in this book is to show you and teach you the more essential hypnosis, and even allow you, if you want, go further on your way to your training as some vital aspects.

To achieve this end, I have developed and epitomized this book Course Practical Hypnosis intended to teach you how to hypnotize professional level, and apply hypnosis in different contexts, situations, environments and varied circumstances, together with your friends, family, known participants, customers or coachee. In this 2nd book you will learn to put into practice what they have learned, and even be fully prepared and ready to make your first therapeutic clinical hypnosis session or your first show of street hypnosis or show. So, without further ado champions and champions, let's start with our first lesson.

Most frequent questions about hypnosis:

Now you ask: You really can learn to hypnotize through an online course or by reading a book? YES; Any apprentice can become and become an excellent hypnotist no need to have special powers or magical supernatural gifts and talents. You just have to study it very carefully, practice it with great discipline and perseverance. And above all know the different and varied "Techniques and Methodologies" you need to know to master every good hypnotist, hypnotist or hypnotherapist.

Myths About Hypnosis and Around:

Is it true that some people are hypnotizable and others not? Every human being is hypnotizable in some way or another, what happens is that not everyone reacts or responds in the same way induction processes; and of course, not all react or respond to the same techniques of hypnosis.

*In other words; my apprentice, "If you can learn to hypnotize, anyone, anytime and anywhere. The issue is not, if you go into hypnosis, the question is, when you enter. Since everyone is hypnotizable if you know the "how" and "what" responds …***NOTE***:* (It should be clarified. At this point, which is the unconscious of the subject which itself decides to accept or not, to the suggestions of the hypnotist If the subject at a given moment, not to be hypnotized, for that person then hypnosis will result, since it is he himself who has voluntarily access inductions the hypnotist and want to do everything that you are giving, and do all that suggests the hypnotist).

Is it true that only weak-willed people can be hypnotized or only can hypnotize weak-minded people? We question this false myth … Until the next question Have you ever thought about the number of people using self-hypnosis, positive suggestions and power of your mind as a means to improve or outdo themselves? In fact, it has been demonstrated, tested and scientifically verified over and over again that the most creative, intuitive, full of imagination and self-reliant people enter into trances HYPNOTIC much faster, more effectively and in some manner more powerful individuals who have doubts or lack of creativity and imagination. Since I repeat, it has been shown scientifically proven that an open mind and a positive attitude is much more powerful, intuitive and resourceful, that endless likely much higher and extraordinary unlimited opens,

Ie champions and champions, that people who go into a hypnotic trance state are not weak-minded in any way; On the contrary, it can be said apprentice, that people who enter hypnosis are more open, receptive, willing and ingenious mind. In other words, they are more susceptible (capable, able, willing, skillful) and responsive to hypnotic trance state. That is, they are more sensitive and lend to receive orders, suggestions, inductions the hypnotist people. And this quality so extraordinarily wonderful my dear readers "is a skill, a natural gift and innate talent". Hypnotizable be, rather than a defect, is an attention span that we should all want to develop.

Is hypnosis dangerous? Apprentice; the act of hypnosis itself is not dangerous. The most recent studies and tests conducted scientifically, along with the experiences of hundreds and thousands of specialists (Hypnotists, Hypnotists, hypnotists and hypnotherapists) it shows us loud and clear that you cannot make an individual under any discipline, either clinical hypnosis, show hypnosis or adopt any behavior contrary to morals, religion and morality; or to do or perform any act of risk that put your life in danger. Since everything (Hypnotist, Hypnotist, hypnotist and hypnotherapist) alone has the power, the unconscious of the subject itself voluntarily deliver him.

<u>Several examples will put</u> If a hypnotist specialist in a show of show you get a subject to behave like a certain animal, and adopt the behavior of a dog, a cat or a chicken, it is because the subject himself knows intuitively unconsciously that this is only a role play (Hypnotist - Participant). Another example: if in a clinical hypnosis session hypnotherapist tells your patient, try to remember a traumatic past experience; and revive it, to change events and able to overcome what has affected him; and the person accepts, and access instructions specialist. It is because he knows and believes that the therapist can help you overcome this situation. What you need to always keep in mind is that no (street Hypnotist or Mesmer show of shows,

<u>FOR EXAMPLE</u>, *my apprentice; If you're not a psychiatrist, psychologist or hypnotherapist entitled, collegial and certificate, you should never make any hypnosis treatment against any addiction, whether to snuff, alcohol, drugs or any other challenge, if not in your area of competence. (Remember: All this treatment should be done by experts and specialists on that topic Although you might think that there is no risk, strongly discouraged its practice by professional and ethical principles.)If you are an expert in* hypnosis Street the contrary or are a Mesmer specialist show of shows, then you should keep your actions to limit what your professional experience and your artistic knowledge will allow, provided they never do or effects an event this outside your professional area of excellence. Ie never prescribe treatment or diagnose disease; since this is not your competition, nor your professional workspace.

Can hypnosis mentally affect in a negative way? Or hypnosis can sometimes be dangerous? This myth is one of the most interesting; For this reason, leave it in last place to explain and understand clearly favorable and unfavorable balanced, negative or positive and reality or fiction of this myth. To begin we can state categorically that the hypnotic act is not dangerous in itself. Experience through the years, and hundreds of scientific medical studies show us decisively that you cannot make an individual (patient or participant) under hypnosis adopt conduct contrary to your moral ethics, principles and values, religious beliefs, morals, ideals or any other thoughts, feelings or actions that violates dignity or put your life at risk or endangered. Consider that the (street hypnotist, the hypnotist show,

If for example a street hypnotist in one of his presentations street manages to make one of its participants fingers, hands or feet sticking, it is because the same participant agreed to the suggestions freely, realizing that these very popular hypnotic phenomena in this types of presentations are conducted through the voluntary participation of the person itself, who know that is only part of a mental game can be swayed by bringing experience as a result favorably achieve the desired hypnotic phenomenon. Similarly, if a hypnotist show gets a subject the public to behave like a dog, cat or any other animal, it is because the person in question knows intuitively and unconsciously that it is a game in which he is the protagonist.

So, if you have to take into account, and I emphasize so important it is. It is that no street hypnotist or hypnotist show should for any reason, reason or circumstance diagnostics or treat diseases without prior knowledge and be authorized for this purpose, as this is solely and exclusively for clinical and hypnotherapists hypnotist's specialist who are empowered and qualified for such therapies and procedures. It is important to note at this point that any diagnosis or treatment should only be carried out by specialists in the subject such as they are, psychiatrists, doctors, psychologists and hypnotherapists. Neither the coach nor the trainer in NLP are empowered to diagnose or treat diseases unless they are properly qualified and authorized to do so,

__To recapitulate__ Apprentice; the hypnotic state does not imply any danger, since hypnosis is a natural state of every human being. If there is any possibility of danger at some point; this could only be married, inadvertently, through unauthorized, negligent and incompetent practice by a hypnotist, Hypnotist, hypnotist and hypnotherapist; exercising the profession without the background needed for making or without a university degree required, if applicable.

1. **Psychological risks** Apprentice; If you're not a psychiatrist, psychologist or hypnotherapist entitled, collegial and certificate and you lack information about the past of the person (you can accentuate an imbalance, but not provoke him.) (You can also provide an excuse to fall into a latent imbalance). For this reason, it is not advisable to practice clinical hypnosis without: Have maintained a previous interview with the subject, have made the medical report, read and complete the therapeutic script with the patient, completing and reviewing the contract or posthypnotic agreement to keep in mind the goals they want to achieve with the session, deepening the reason for the consultation or session, ask questions on the subject to locate possible psychological and physiological problems, if any, detect fears, traumas, phobias, expectations, desires and interests, etc.

In conclusion My apprentice, there is no inherent danger in the practice of hypnosis, but slight risks associated with incompetence of the hypnotist. All these risks can INSIST avoided by simply: Make a previous interview, have a pre-hypnotic chat with or participant, write the medical report or read and complete therapeutic script with the patient, completing and reviewing the contract or posthypnotic agreement to keep in mind the goals they want to achieve with the session, deepening the reason for the consultation or session, ask questions on the subject to locate possible psychological and physiological problems, if any, detect fears, traumas, phobias, expectations, desires and interests, etc.

Do you understand what I'm saying? In doing all this my apprentice, you'll not only prevent any problems with time, but above all you can come on and cover any expectation, positioning yourself as an expert and specialist in the field; consolidate your image as Hypnotist, Hypnotist, hypnotist or hypnotherapist. It is clear that having a profile of the staff concerned who go to work, you will have more advantages, if not you would fulfill with these initial procedures do I know you understand? You are an apprentice agreement, which, having more information, more likely to have success in carrying out your therapeutic clinical hypnosis sessions and more likely to have success to make your shows of street hypnosis or show. Are you clear on this truth? REMEMBER THAT:

Now my apprentice; I would like to make two (2) commitments: (Following this course Hypnosis Practice and apply these techniques of hypnosis in your therapeutic clinical sessions or show of street hypnosis or show, it implies that "AGREE 100%" each of these two (2) conditions.)

COMMITMENTS AND CONDITIONS

1 You get 100% responsible for the welfare of the hypnotized, locking always focused on the principles and moral values, with the highest standards of ethics and professionalism. (If you follow to the letter all this course of practice hypnosis with all recommendations of what you can do; And all recommendations you owe, and you have to avoid I can assure apprentice in your actual practice, it will never happen anything that is out of reach. Since, to properly pay prompt attention to my recommendations, you'll be more prepared and ready to avoid, prevent or solve any problems that it occurs to you) Do you agree?

2nd You should never practice any of the techniques discussed in this course of practice hypnosis until you acquire all the techniques necessary skills, mastered and basic methodologies recommended in hypnosis, and especially you have reached the part where you can practice hypnosis effectively and you can perform all procedures correctly. This is the most important part ... "My apprentice; before starting to hypnotize, you have to know all the steps that must be taken to hypnosis to be successful. " To achieve this goal, we must be prepared, ready and alert to any possible "danger", "risk" or "event" that might arise, and perfectly master the techniques of suggestion and fascination.

It's not enough; only to provide texts hypnosis techniques, and to read them hypnotized. (One must know how to properly use the tone of our voice, we must know that rhythm, beat and style must be used in each state and levels of hypnosis, and recognize the stage where we are. We have to go running tests of suggestibility, covert tests, inductions, convencers and downriggers of hypnotic states. to induce further, creating hypnotic phenomena, perform post-hypnotic suggestion, and successfully complete the procedures of awakening.

You should also increase Circle of Power or Strength Level one (FP1, FP2 and FP3) to a higher level of authority or higher (FP4, FP5) and above. Similarly, way apprentice; You must learn to choose hypnotic trance states that want to achieve according to the above stated objectives, as well as master (STATE HIPNOIDAL or IncantationZ0 and Z1, TRANCE HYPNOTIC SLIGHT or Superficial Z1, MEDIUM or cataleptic HYPNOTIC TRANCE Z1 and Z2 or Z2 somnambulic THRESHOLD HYPNOTIC TRANCE as appropriate, etc.).

Apprentice; above all we must learn to be patient, and do things well done. (That is, do the right things correctly) For example, if you try to hypnotize a person (without being properly prepared and trained for this purpose) by reading only a few hypnosis techniques that person. I can assure you that the failure rate will be around 99, 99%. Bringing as unfavorable consequences for you, that the unconscious of the subject who had tried to hypnotize assume you do not know. in the worst case, and we most affect most all specialists and professional's hypnosis, it is to think of anyone that hypnosis is not real, making it harder for an upcoming session of hypnosis therapy clinic level professional,

So, while having all the best hypnosis techniques by hand, first you must keep them, until the right time to test them. Do you understand what I'm trying to tell you? You know apprentice, that everything has its time, and every action has its time. I promise you, if you put interest and exert the necessary once you can control "everything" discipline, you get a 90% chance of success by practicing hypnosis and do it properly.

> **APPRENTICE, I have seen that this course of practice hypnosis follows from all over the world. For that reason; Importantly, in some countries, the practice of hypnosis is prohibited and punished (banned or punishable by law). Such as happens in cases of countries such as England, among others. So, make sure that in your country HYPNOSIS practice is legal, so you can practice hypnosis.**

SYNTHESIS:

Until this part of the course, you must have learned that:

✓ *Everyone can hypnotize, to follow this course if he tries.*
✓ *Anyone can become a good professional hypnotist.*
✓ *Everyone is, and can be hypnotized; knowing how, and which responds at a time or a certain circumstance.*
✓ *Hypnosis itself is harmless and does not imply any danger.*
✓ *Risks of hypnosis, when used inappropriately.*
✓ *Do not practice hypnosis techniques until instructed.*
✓ *You agree to comply and follow faithfully the two (2) commitments and conditions.*
✓ *You must be entitled, collegiate and university studies to work professionally as a clinical hypnotist or hypnotherapist.*
✓ *What are some tips to consider before, during and after practice our hypnosis session?*
✓ *You can become the best street hypnotist or the best hypnotist show if you put your mind and acquire prior knowledge.*

EXERCISES:

To see that you understand everything, here are a series of exercises:

Is every person can hypnotize, to follow this course if you propose?
R) =

Anyone can become a good professional hypnotist?
R) =

Everybody is, and can be hypnotized? Explain why
R) =

Does Hypnosis itself is harmless and does not imply any danger?
Explain why
R) =

What if there was any risk in hypnosis which would be the reason that may have caused?
R) =

What are some risks of hypnosis, when used inappropriately?
R) =

What are some tips to consider before, during and after practice our hypnosis session?
R) =

What you need to know, know and master to be an excellent hypnotist and bring your practices and hypnosis sessions to the next level?
R) =

¿As we have studied, what are the 4 types of titles attributed to different specialists and experts in the practice of hypnosis?
R) =

Do you accept 100% faithfully fulfill the two (2) commitments and conditions to continue advancing the online course?
R) =

Should you be entitled, collegiate and university studies to work professionally as a clinical hypnotist or hypnotherapist?
R) =

Can you become the best street hypnotist or the best hypnotist show if you put your mind and acquire prior knowledge?
R) =

WHAT IS THE MOST IMPORTANT THING YOU HAVE LEARNED IN THIS LESSON?
R) =

Good **LEARNERS**, This **It has been all for now!**... wuao interesting everything we learned in this first lesson, right? **I HOPE YOU HAVE LIKED this first introductory chapter**... Good luck with the exercises, I know I will answer very well. If you have any questions to answer the questionnaire, *calmed down (The answers to these questions are available on the next page) If there is something that may not understand; quiet is normal, when you start a new learning*:). Good; keep in mind that, *"If you have any questions, you can "directly write me Email" (E-mail).*

MásterCoach.YlichTarazona@gmail.com
http://www.reingenieriamentalconpnl.com

If you enjoyed this workshop hypnosis, and want to "help" with your contribution, to support me to continue doing this wonderful work, which, with love, prepared for you. You can do this through the following link.

http://bit.ly/PaypalDonación
Thank you for your contribution

THE POWER OF PURPOSE: *"Knowing what the purpose that gives meaning to our existence, is what ultimately allows us to rediscover why we are here and we are born. Let us remember that we are all born with a purpose, all have a mission. And when we discover and we pursue it, this will not only give meaning to our existence, but open endless chances to take us straight to our destination. "- YLICH TARAZONA. -*

<u>Solutions to Exercises Lesson Previous:</u>

Is every person can hypnotize, to follow this course if you propose?
R) = SI

Anyone can become a good professional hypnotist?
R) = SI

Everybody is, and can be hypnotized? Explain why
R) = Because knowing how and to which responds at a certain time or circumstance a person, we can suggest him and hypnotize you by following these principles. You can learn to hypnotize, anyone, anytime and anywhere. The issue is not, if you go into hypnosis, the question is, when you enter. Since everyone is hypnotizable if you know the "how" and "what" answers.

Does Hypnosis itself is harmless and does not imply any danger? Explain why
R) = The hypnotic state does not imply any danger, since hypnosis is a natural state of every human being.

What if there was any risk in hypnosis which would be the reason that may have caused?
R) = If there is any possibility of danger at some point; this could only be married, through unauthorized, negligent and incompetent practice by a Hypnotist, Mesmer, hypnologist and hipnoterapeuta; exercising without the background needed for making or without a university degree required, if applicable.

What are some risks of hypnosis, when used inappropriately?
R) = If you're not a psychiatrist, psychologist or hypnotherapist entitled, collegial and certificate and you lack information about the past of the person (can accentuate an imbalance, but not provoke him.) You can also provide an excuse to fall into a latent imbalance.

What are some tips to consider before, during and after practice our hypnosis session?
R) = It is advisable to practice clinical hypnosis without: Have maintained a previous interview with the subject, have made the medical report, read and complete the therapeutic script with the patient, fill the contract or posthypnotic agreement to keep in mind the goals they want achieve with the session, deepening the reason for the consultation or session, ask questions on the subject to locate possible psychological and physiological problems, if any, detect fears, traumas, phobias, expectations, desires and interests, etc.

What you need to know, know and master to be an excellent hypnotist and bring your practices and hypnosis sessions to the next level?

R) = One must know how to properly use the tone of our voice, we must know that rhythm, beat and style there to be employed in each state, and recognize the stage where we are, go running tests of suggestibility tests covert, inductions, convencers and downriggers of hypnotic states, Induce, deepen, creating hypnotic phenomena, perform post-hypnotic suggestion, successfully complete the procedures of awakening, increase Circle of Power or Strength Level one (FP1, FP2 and FP3) a Mayor Authority level or higher FP5 and above, choose hypnotic trance state we want to achieve our goals according to (STATE HIPNOIDAL or Z0 and Z1 Incantation, mild hypnotic trance Superficial Z1,HYPNOTIC TRANCE MEDIUM or cataleptic Z1 and Z2 or Z2 somnambulistic THRESHOLD HYPNOTIC TRANCE as appropriate.

¿As we have studied, what are the 4 types of titles attributed to different specialists and experts in the practice of hypnosis?

R) = The 4 types of titles attributed to different specialists and experts in the practice of hypnosis are:

✓ **HYPNOTIST** = *Applied to Hypnotist Street.*
✓ **HYPNOTIST** = *Applied to Mesmer in Show of Shows.*
✓ **hypnologist CLINICAL** = *Applied professional in the practice of hypnosis clinic.*
✓ **hypnotherapist** = *Applied to Professional practice therapies, hypnotherapy sessions.*

Do you accept 100% faithfully fulfill the two (2) commitments and conditions to continue advancing the online course?

R) = Yes, I agree 100% faithfully fulfill the "2 Commitments and Conditions" to move forward the online course.

Should you be entitled, collegiate and university studies to work professionally as a clinical hypnotist or hypnotherapist?

R) = SI

Can you become the best street hypnotist or the best hypnotist show if you put your mind and acquire prior knowledge?

R) = SI

WHAT IS THE MOST IMPORTANT THING YOU HAVE LEARNED IN THIS LESSON?

R) = "Free Reply" Each participant may have to answer this question as you have learned and what they would like to share with the facilitator.

<u>**IMPORTANT**</u>: Remember apprentice, who, to the next level of this practice hypnosis course, I have prepared, it epitomized designed for you. It implies that you have accepted 100% the conditions and commitments mentioned above on Page 20. Well if so, let's continue ... ^ _ ^

MásterCoach.YlichTarazona@gmail.com
http://www.reingenieriamentalconpnl.com

If you enjoyed this workshop hypnosis, and want to "help" with your contribution, to support me to continue doing this wonderful work, which, with love, prepared for you. You can do this through the following link.

http://bit.ly/PaypalDonación
Thank you for your contribution

THE POWER OF PURPOSE *(Part Two): "To know where we are going, it is important and essential in our path to personal excellence, have a north set allows us to walk in the right direction, knowing where we allow us to set the path and the coordinates for which we must lead and guide us to reach our destination. In other words, be clear about our mission in life and know what is the purpose that gives meaning to our existence, is what allows us to finally rediscover why we are here and we are born. Let us remember that we are all born with a purpose, we all have a mission and when we discover and we pursue it, this will not only give meaning to our existence, but open endless chances to take us straight to our destination ". YLICH TARAZONA*

CHAPTER SECOND: STATEMENTS OF HYPNOSIS AND DEPTH LEVELS

Hello such apprentice, we have come to the second part of this course of practice hypnosis. In this lesson we will learn on the levels of hypnosis.

The three (3) STATEMENTS OF HYPNOSIS:

To begin this lesson, we will use the classification of Eric Barone.

Let us classify STATES HYPNOSIS as "types" of accepted suggestions, their circle of power or force level, characteristics and frequency levels or brain waves presented in each particular state. In depth order, they are: Z1 and Z2 "(The normal state would be the Z0 and would not state the Z3).

The Z0 State (Normal)

In the beginning of the hypnosis session the subject (viewer) patient or participant, it is in the NORMAL STATE OF ALERT or wakeful state (Z0). This conscious state is characterized by a high level of frequency or brain waves in neuronal activity BETA ranging from 14 to 28 Hz (cycles per second or cps)

This Z0 state is the open expression of feelings and sensory perceptions (VAK "O and G") Visual, auditory and sensory "Kinesthetic". This Z0 state can receive and accept simple suggestions, positive affirmations, inductions and hypnotic patterns through conversational hypnosis of a circle power level Force or Authority Level "FP0".

The Z0 state is conducive to focus on a specific activity, it is characterized by the expression of verbal and nonverbal communication, memory, emotions, memories, instincts, attention, thoughts, desires, actions and knowledge. It features remain fully alert with 5 active senses (sight, hearing, touch, taste and smell).

The State Z1 (mild)

This Z1 (mild) state is divided into "(2 levels)" state or level HIPNOIDAL Charm and level HYPNOTIC TRANCE SLIGHT or Superficial.

The state Z1, Level HIPNOIDAL or Incantation. Is semi-conscious state, characterized by decreasing the frequency levels or brain waves in neuronal activity ALPHA / ALPHA ranging from 8 to 13 Hz (cycles per second or cps).

State Z1 TRANCE LIGHT conducive to start making practice self-hypnosis and hypnosis. It is a favorable state to receive and accept simple suggestions, positive affirmations, progressive inductions and hypnotic patterns basic circle power level Force or Authority Level "FP1" and "FP2". In this state Z1 Level "HIPNOIDAL or Incantation" the subject (viewer) patient or participant is aware of everything that happens in their environment, so sometimes I could doubt his STATE OF TRANCE HYPNOTIC HIPNOIDAL or Incantation, and listening the hypnotist and perceives everything that happens in their surroundings and environment around him. But upon awakening; Mostly they will evaluate the time incorrectly believe that it's been ten minutes when in fact it's been a much greater perceived time. This state Z1 Level "HIPNOIDAL or Incantation" makes us more suggestible to emotions and feelings.

This hypnotic state Z1 occurs naturally or can be created or stimulated through several sensory stimuli. FOR EXAMPLE:
- ✓ *Seeing a movie, going to the movies, listen to certain music.*
- ✓ *While we recite a prayer or a mantra.*
- ✓ *While we dive into reading a good book.*
- ✓ *When we are in love - infatuation or enchantment.*
- ✓ *When we have a slight loss of sense of time.*
- ✓ *When we receptiveness to certain advertising or publicity.*
- ✓ *It manifests when we daydream or visualize.*
- ✓ *While a class or witness heard a talk or conference.*

It is characterized by the following HYPNOTICS PHENOMENA
- ✓ *Mental relaxation*
- ✓ *Physical relaxation*
- ✓ *Partial decreased breathing*
- ✓ *Partial decreased pulse or heartbeat*
- ✓ *Feeling mild lethargy*
- ✓ *Feeling faint catalepsy*
- ✓ *Partial closure of eyes*
- ✓ *Increased number of flutter*
- ✓ *Partial sluggishness of mind*

As this state Z1 is very unstable, and the individual always tends to return to normal waking state. For this reason, it is advisable that during this period, the hypnotist, Hypnotist, hypnotist or hypnotherapist must take into account the switch and deepen techniques and sound, tactile and visual methodologies, to bring the person to the next level Z1 state. The Superficial mild hypnotic trance. Semi-conscious state, characterized by a further decrease of the frequency levels or brain waves in neuronal activity ZETA / THETA ranging from 6 to 7 Hz (cycles per second or cps).

This state Z1 the hypnotic trance mild Superficial is conducive to accept and receive a larger amount and direct suggestions and suggestive inductions mild hypnotic patterns and progressive commands a circle power Strength Level or Level of Authority "FP3" and " FP4 ".

In this state, the subject is aware of everything happening around him, so sometimes I could also doubt under the influence of state level TRANCE HYPNOTIC mild Superficial, but the awakening will evaluate the time has quickly passed without realizing it at all. He'll have spent time, when in fact it has been perceived much more.

The state level Z1 HYPNOTIC TRANCE mild Superficial is conducive to practice relaxation, meditation, concentration and developing states excellence through hypnosis. This state is also conducive to practice intimacy and sexual relations to a higher level multiorgasmic type Tibetan tantric sex or Hindu sex "Kama Sutra".

*State **ONIRICAL** or state **TWILIGHT** conducive to stimulate and create lucid dreams, astral travel or lead-body experiences. State conducive to start Influence and induce positive changes in our thoughts, feelings, behaviors and habits.*

It is characterized by the following HYPNOTICS PHENOMENA
- ✓ *Greater control of emotions and feelings*
- ✓ *Decreased breathing, this slows*
- ✓ *gradual decrease of the pulse or heart rate*
- ✓ *Feeling of lethargy or mental and physical sluggishness*
- ✓ *Ocular sensation catalepsy and tips*
    - ✓ *Close your eyes and increase the number of flutter*
- ✓ *Increased empathy, allowing create greater rapport in therapeutic hypnosis sessions or clinical hypnosis shows*
- ✓ *The person becomes more susceptible to suggestions and inductions being more conducive to receiving and accepting direct orders*
- ✓ *State conducive to practicing hypnosis sessions, coaching and NLP among other alternative practices such as reiki, yoga, tai chi or acupuncture.*
- ✓ *Increased capacity Reflex (Martial Arts)*
- ✓ *Been supportive and very effective to program the mind to brain reengineering, practice hypnopedia, Self-hypnosis, auto-suggestion, self-display or learn or practice some new language or skill.*

The suggestions ACCEPTED IN THIS STATE MUST BE POSITIVE, AFFIRMATIVE AND PROGRESSIVE suggestions. The degree of CIRCLE POWER or force level Z1 is (FP2 and FP3), and authority level or upper level to FP4 "{(We discuss types of suggestion as grades or levels of authority)}". To continue, taking as an example: that of a smoker who has decided to quit. Possible suggestions in the state Z1 are: From now on you have the desire and the desire to breathe better and better every day from now feel your lungs clear, and free allowing you to breathe better every day, your desire to smoking decreases more and more with each passing day anxiety smoking gradually diminishes, and it makes you feel better and better, both mentally and physically.

The State Z2 (deep)

This Z2 (light) state is divided into "(2 levels)" HYPNOTIC TRANCE MEDIUM or catalepsy and somnambulism THRESHOLD HYPNOTIC TRANCE.

The state Z2, Level MEDIUM or cataleptic HYPNOTIC TRANCE. It is the largest state of semi-consciousness, characterized by a further decrease of the frequency levels or brain waves in neuronal activity ZETA / THETA ranging from 4 to 5 Hz (cycles per second or cps) *outwardly perceptible.*

The Z2 state Level hypnotic trance MEDIUM or cataleptic is suitable to receive and accept a greater number of suggestions, inductions and direct subjective orders through patterns and hypnotic commands a circle power Strength Level or Level of Authority "FP5 "and" FP6 ".

It is characterized by the following HYPNOTICS PHENOMENA
✓   It allows the subject to accept inhibitions. (Suggestions Ban)
✓   *Hypnotic produce and generate phenomenon such as: Anesthesia and Analgesia Low and Medium (Grace and susceptible to alleviate and control some degree of pain capacity) Effect fakir - transferred needle, local surgical anesthesia.*
✓   *Amnesia light and medium, ability to forget certain ideas or simple, such as names, dates, numbers, colors, smells, tastes and events.*
✓   *Hypnotic phenomenon Lethargy, Catalepsy and cataleptic Middle Catatonic*
✓   *Ability to maintain Hypnotic Trance Medium or cataleptic, either with eyes open or closed.*
✓   *This status Hypnotic or cataleptic Middle It allows the subject to accept an inhibition (A slight ban) start leaving such a bad habit.*
✓   *ONIRICAL state or state TWILIGHT conducive to stimulate, create maintain lucid dreams, astral travel and extra cause bodily experiences.*
✓   *Multisensory hallucinations visual, auditory and kinesthetic, olfactory and gustatory*
✓   *Ability to enter and maintain deep levels of relaxation, meditation, concentration and Hiper Suggestibility.*

The state Z2, Level threshold or somnambulistic hypnotic trance. State is greater hypnotic trance reached Z2, and is characterized by a greater degree in reducing the frequency levels or brain waves in neuronal activity DELTA ranging from 0.5 to 3 Hz or (cycles per second or cps), which is externally perceptible clarity compared to previous states.

The Z2 state level hypnotic trance THRESHOLD or somnambulistic is suitable to receive and accept a greater number of suggestions, inductions and subjective direct orders through patterns and hypnotic commands a circle power Strength Level or Level of Authority "FP7 "and" FP8 ".

It is characterized by the following HYPNOTICS PHENOMENA
✓　This status hypnotic somnambulistic It allows the subject to accept inhibitions (A mid- and high-ban) stop or control such a bad habit.
State conducive to the practice of Sessions and Show, Regressions and trances.
✓　*State conducive to creating hypnotic phenomena and stimulate "Hyper - suggestibility"" Hyper-creativity "and" hyper-concentration* " **allowing the emergence of ideo motor responses, sensory ideo, and ideo-emotional** *amplifying the response levels and deepening the evocative experiences and sensory, physical and mental extra.*
✓　Ability to develop Phenomenon Hypnotic Analgesia and Anesthesia moderate, overall pain control, ability to walk on burning coals, traversed with pins and tolerance have contact with fire and ice.
✓　Amnesia develop the ability to forget situations, memories, events, phobias, fears and traumas.
✓　Hypnotic phenomenon Lethargy, Catalepsy and Catatonic moderate and high cataleptic limbs or entire body.
✓　Ability to maintain Hypnotic Trance with eyes open or closed and develop the ability to maintain hypnotic phenomena.
✓　**State of hyper - suggestibility** "It is a superior amplification response or downrigger the suggestive experiences or state of hyper concentration and total relaxation that is metaphorically associated with deep slumber, the latter called hypnotic trance state.
✓　Hallucinations multisensory medium, high and you moderate - visual, auditory and kinesthetic, olfactory and gustatory. (See things that really do not see, hear things that actually feel sensations, feelings and physical contacts that are not really real, smell and taste smells or tastes that do not actually exist in the real physical world do not listen)
✓　Ability to consciously control heart rhythm, deep breathing or lethargic and voluntarily control body levels body to withstand high or low temperatures.
✓　higher level of control extended trance and hypnotic phenomena and the state of somnambulism even with open eyes.
✓　*Development capacity* **xenoglossia** *which it is the ability or paranormal phenomenon hypnotic speaking unknown languages and languages.*
✓　*Capacity* **NOESIOLOGY** *which it is the ability of healing with thought. Greek noesis: action of thinking, and healing therapy.*

✓ ***psychographics*** *psychic ability of a person who writes letters without being aware. The person says the words were written by the subconscious, by a spirit or supernatural forces related to hypnosis.*

✓ *Hypnotic ability to develop phenomena as regressions, distortion or disassociation of time and space, body, visual or auditory illusions, deep meditation, and mystical experiences assumptions such as clairvoyance. And even lucid dreams and astral travel.*

In this state Z2, Level threshold or somnambulistic hypnotic trance, the subject has numbed their critical faculties ("Critical Factor of Mind"). Continues to communicate and continues to receive messages from the outside world, but when you wake up temporarily recalled some events, situations, memories, experiences and experiences that have happened in certain contexts. Saying that he erases or forget time certain events, I mean that when I wake up the subject and return to your state of alertness (alertness or wakefulness), if we asked you to tell us everything you remember from the beginning hypnosis session, will remember only so far before, what brought him into the state of deep hypnotic trance.

Compared to the (state Z1), this state Z2 allows the subject to accept orders from a higher degree of CIRCLE or power level Force (FP7 and FP8), and a higher level of authority or higher FP9 and above. In the state Z2 the subject accepts orders, suggestions, commands and hypnotic inductions inhibition patterns. An order, suggestion and hypnotic induction prohibition also incorporates quite well in his unconscious and deeply into their behavior. In the case of smoking the previous example: THIS STATE Z2 ALLOW SUGGESTIONS INHIBITION AND BANS together to positive, affirmative, progressive inductions as: From now on, you feel so good about yourself, which makes you easy to quit smoking, each passing day you feel so good,

The Z3 (deep) state does not serve hypnosis

The Z3 (deep) state is known as fugue state. Because when a person refuses to accept the reality mostly caused by a traumatic process or state of emotional shock, and you cannot wake up to reality, it takes refuge in a deeper state, the Z3, as a preventive measure.

In this state Z3, the subject loses consciousness; He has broken all ties with the outside world; not hear anything consciously and behaves as if anesthetized, for that reason this state Z3 is not conducive to hypnosis.

The Z3 STATE (It's a very deep state of Reverie); If this phenomenon happens, you will notice very easily, seeing that the subject does not react to our hypnotic suggestions, and we can even see it even really sleep (literal or physiologically) talking. In this state Z3 (Condition Very Deep Dream), the subject even once awakes, he cannot remember anything that has happened at this stage. (Although it reminds us) and the reason is simple and easy "It was because he fell asleep, and slept as is logical, not only receives no hypnotic order, but remember nothing of what he says, even if it made any involuntary action during sleep "...

This is logical, and it is very clear. It's like trying to remind a SLEEP (person who talks and walks while asleep) to remember what he did or said while he was asleep. Is it impossible, right? good the same thing happens in this STATE Z3 (Very Deep State of Dream).

SYNTHESIS:

Until this part of the course, you should have learned:

The three states and levels of hypnosis are: Z1 (mild), Z2 (deep), Z3 (very deep)

Z1: The hypnotized person thinks that he has not yet fallen under the effect of hypnosis, he only accepts positive, affirmative or progressive suggestions.
Z2: His critical faculties diminish, he does not usually remember anything of what happens, this state allows the subject to accept an inhibition. (A prohibition)
Z3: State of escape because he refuses a suggestion or does not manage to wake up, there is no relationship with the hypnotized, he does not listen. (To wake him up, he would wake up like anyone with normal sleep.)

We also learned the states and the degrees or levels of Hypnosis

STATE OF VIGIL "Z0" - Present here and now

BETA STATE = Between 14 to 28 Hz or (cycles per second or cps)
Receive and accept simple suggestions, positive affirmations, inductions and patterns through the conversational hypnosis of a POWER CIRCLE, Force Level or Authority Level "FP0". It is characterized by staying fully awake, alert and with the 5 active senses (sight, hearing, touch, taste and smell).

STATE HIPNOIDAL *or Incantation Z0 and Z1.*

STATE ALPHA / ALPHA = 8 to 13 Hz or (cycles per second or cps)

LIGHTWEIGHT trancelike state conducive to start performing self-hypnosis, hypnosis practice and is a favorable state to receive and accept simple suggestions, positive affirmations, progressive inductions and hypnotic patterns basic circle power or force level Authority Level "FP1" and "FP2".

hypnotic state that occurs naturally or created, for example:

- ✓ Seeing a movie, going to the movies, listen to certain music.
- ✓ While we recite a prayer or a mantra.
- ✓ While we dive into reading a good book.
- ✓ When we are in love - infatuation or enchantment.

It is characterized by the following HYPNOTICS PHENOMENA

- ✓ Mental relaxation
- ✓ Physical relaxation
- ✓ Partial decreased breathing
- ✓ Partial decreased pulse or heartbeat
- ✓ Feeling mild lethargy
- ✓ Feeling faint catalepsy

Superficial HYPNOTIC TRANCE MILD or Z1.

STATE ZETA / THETA = 4 to 7 Hz or (cycles per second or cps)

It is conducive to accept and receive a larger amount and direct suggestions and mild suggestive inductions and hypnotic patterns and commands a circle progressive power level Force or Authority Level "FP3" and "FP4".

It is characterized by the following HYPNOTICS PHENOMENA

- ✓ Greater control of emotions and feelings
- ✓ Decreased breathing, this slows
- ✓ gradual decrease of the pulse or heart rate
- ✓ Feeling of lethargy or mental and physical sluggishness
- ✓ Ocular sensation catalepsy and tips
- ✓ Close your eyes and increase the number of flutter

HYPNOTIC TRANCE MEDIUM or cataleptic Z1 and Z2.

STATE ZETA / THETA = 4 to 7 Hz or (cycles per second)

It is suitable to receive and accept a greater number of suggestions, inductions and direct through hypnotic patterns circle power level Force or Authority Level "FP5" and "FP6" subjective orders.

It is characterized by the following HYPNOTICS PHENOMENA

- ✓ Hypnotic phenomenon Anesthesia and Analgesia Low and Medium (tolerance and capacity susceptible to relieve and control certain degree of pain) Effect Fakir - carried over needle, local surgical anesthesia.
- ✓ Amnesia light and medium, ability to forget certain ideas or simple, such as names, dates, numbers, colors, smells, tastes and events.
- ✓ Ability to maintain Hypnotic Trance Medium or cataleptic, either with eyes open or closed.

✓   This status Hypnotic or cataleptic Middle It allows the subject to accept an inhibition (A slight ban) start leaving such a bad habit.

HYPNOTIC TRANCE THRESHOLD somnambulistic or somnambulistic Z2. STATE DELTA = 0.5 to 3 Hz Between *or* **(Cycles per second or cps),**
It is suitable to receive and accept a greater number of suggestions, inductions and subjective through hypnotic patterns and commands a circle power level Force or Authority Level "FP7" and "FP8" direct orders.
It is characterized by the following HYPNOTICS PHENOMENA
✓   *State conducive to creating hypnotic phenomena and stimulate "Hyper - suggestibility"" Hyper-creativity "and" hyper-concentration "* **allowing the emergence of ideo motor responses, sensory ideo, and ideo-emotional** *amplifying the response levels and deepening the evocative experiences and sensory, physical and mental extra.*
✓   Ability to develop Phenomenon Hypnotic Analgesia and Anesthesia moderate, overall pain control, ability to walk on burning coals, traversed with pins and tolerance have contact with fire and ice.
✓   Hypnotic phenomenon Lethargy, Catalepsy and Catatonic moderate and high cataleptic limbs or entire body.
✓   **State of hyper - suggestibility** "It is a superior amplification response or downrigger the suggestive experiences or state of hyper concentration and total relaxation that is metaphorically associated with deep slumber, the latter called hypnotic trance state.

EXERCISES:

To see that you understand everything, here are a series of exercises:

1)   Under what we have studied classification (according to accepted suggestion) how many states we can find a hypnotized person? Name them:
R) =

2)   What kind of suggestions are accepted in the Z1 state? What are the levels of this state and what are some of its features? P**O**WER circulated, Strength Level or Level of Authority?
R) =

3)   What kind of suggestions are accepted in the Z2 state? What are the levels of this state and what are some of its features? P**O**WER circulated, Strength Level or Level of Authority?
R) =

4)   What kind of suggestions are accepted in the state Z3?
R) =

5) Imagine that we want to hypnotize a person, we do not have much time, so we need to know the minimum state where we throw the subject to accept each of the following suggestions:

<u>A.</u> *Every night when you lie on your bed, you will feel very relaxed, more relaxed, and want to sleep, because the only way you can rest and prepare for the next day ... Z1*

<u>B.</u> *Whenever you sit down to study, you will feel very relaxed, and see how well you assimilate every page you read, will cost less memorize Z1 ...*

<u>C.</u> *Every night when you lie on your bed, you'll see how you fall into a deep sleep. There will be nothing to be concerned about. Although try to stay awake, your eyes will close and you can rest peacefully that night Z2 ...*

6) Write the suggestions you could say the Z1 and Z2 been a person who wants to stop being afraid of cats:

R) =

7) WHAT IS THE MOST IMPORTANT THING YOU HAVE LEARNED IN THIS LESSON?

R) =

Good LEARNERS, we have **Finished the second chapter**! This interesting course Hypnosis Practice. Again, very lucky with the exercises. Remember, if you have any questions to answer the questionnaire relax, relax. *(The answers to these questions are available on the next page)* If there is something that may not yet understand; quiet as I see how slowly lapsing as you read you will understand "I promise "*If you have any questions, you can "email me directly to my mail (E-mail)"*.

MásterCoach.YlichTarazona@gmail.com
http://www.reingenieriamentalconpnl.com

If you enjoyed this workshop hypnosis, and want to "help" with your contribution, to support me to continue doing this wonderful work, which, with love, prepared for you. You can do this through the following link.

http://bit.ly/PaypalDonación
Thank you for your contribution

"I firmly believe that there is within the interior of each of us a seed of greatness and lies a vast reservoir of unlimited potential and usually remain dormant skills; waiting to be discovered and developed, to blossom into our outer world. When each of us awaken the individual potential, we rediscover what our mission and purpose that gives meaning to our lives, we will open the way to a new awakening conscious what I call reinventing and reengineering PERSONAL "-. YLICH TARAZONA. -

Solutions to Exercises Lesson Previous:

1) Under what we have studied classification (according to accepted suggestion) how many states we can find a hypnotized person? Name them:
R) = Z1 and Z2. It could be considered the normal state as Z0 and Z3 as non-hypnotic state

2) What kind of suggestions are accepted in the Z1 state?
R) = Only accepts positive, affirmative and progressive suggestions.
R) = STATE HIPNOIDAL Z0 and Z1 or Incantation.
R) STATE = ALPHA / ALPHA = Between 8-13 *Hz or* **(Cycles per second or cps)**
R) = *LIGHTWEIGHT trancelike state conducive to start performing self-hypnosis, hypnosis practice and is a favorable state to receive and accept simple suggestions, positive affirmations, progressive inductions and hypnotic patterns basic circle power or force level Authority Level* "FP1" *and* "FP2".
R) = Hypnotic state that occurs naturally or created, for example:
✓   Seeing a movie, going to the movies, listen to certain music.
✓   While we recite a prayer or a mantra.
✓   While we dive into reading a good book.
✓   When we are in love - infatuation or enchantment.
It is characterized by the following HYPNOTICS PHENOMENA
✓   Mental relaxation
✓   Physical relaxation
✓   Partial decreased breathing
✓   Partial decreased pulse or heartbeat
✓   Feeling mild lethargy
✓   Feeling faint catalepsy
****
R) = This state allows the subject to accept inhibition. (A ban)
R) = SLIGHT HYPNOTIC TRANCE or Superficial Z1.
R) = STATE ZETA / THETA = 4 to 7 *Hz or* **(Cycles per second or cps)**
R) = Is conducive to accept and receive a larger amount and direct and mild suggestive inductions and hypnotic patterns and commands a circle progressive power Strength Level or Level of Authority "FP3" and "FP4" suggestions.
R) = It is characterized by the following HYPNOTICS PHENOMENA
✓   Greater control of emotions and feelings
✓   Decreased breathing, this slows
✓   gradual decrease of the pulse or heart rate
✓   Feeling of lethargy or mental and physical sluggishness
✓   Ocular sensation catalepsy and tips
Close your eyes and increase the number of flutter

3) What kind of suggestions are accepted in the Z2 state?
R) = MEDIUM or cataleptic HYPNOTIC TRANCE Z1 and Z2.
R) = STATE ZETA / THETA = 4 to 7 *Hz or* **(Cycles per second)**

R) = It is suitable to receive and accept a greater number of suggestions, inductions and direct subjective orders through hypnotic patterns circle power Strength Level or Level of Authority "FP5" and "FP6".

R) = It is characterized by the following HYPNOTICS PHENOMENA

✓ Hypnotic phenomenon Anesthesia and Analgesia Low and Medium (tolerance and capacity susceptible to relieve and control certain degree of pain) Effect Fakir - carried over needle, local surgical anesthesia.

✓ Amnesia light and medium, ability to forget certain ideas or simple, such as names, dates, numbers, colors, smells, tastes and events.

✓ Ability to maintain Hypnotic Trance Medium or cataleptic, either with eyes open or closed.

✓ This status Hypnotic or cataleptic Middle It allows the subject to accept an inhibition (A slight ban) start leaving such a bad habit.

****

R) = THRESHOLD somnambulic HYPNOTIC TRANCE or somnambulism Z2.

R) = STATE DELTA = Between 0.5 to 3 *Hz or* **(Cycles per second or cps)**,

R) = It is suitable to receive and accept a greater number of suggestions, inductions and subjective direct orders via hypnotic patterns and commands a circle power level Force or Authority Level "FP7" and "FP8".

R) = It is characterized by the following HYPNOTICS PHENOMENA

✓ *State conducive to creating hypnotic phenomena and stimulate "Hyper - suggestibility"" Hyper-creativity "and" hyper-concentration "* **allowing the emergence of ideo motor responses, sensory ideo, and ideo-emotional** *amplifying the response levels and deepening the evocative experiences and sensory, physical and mental extra.*

✓ Ability to develop Phenomenon Hypnotic Analgesia and Anesthesia moderate, overall pain control, ability to walk on burning coals, traversed with pins and tolerance have contact with fire and ice.

✓ Hypnotic phenomenon Lethargy, Catalepsy and Catatonic moderate and high cataleptic limbs or entire body.

✓ **State of hyper - suggestibility** "It is a superior amplification response or downrigger the suggestive experiences or state of hyper concentration and total relaxation that is metaphorically associated with deep slumber, the latter called hypnotic trance state.

4) What kind of suggestions are accepted in the state Z3?

R) = No relation to the hypnotized, does not listen. Does not accept any suggestion.

5) Imagine that we want to hypnotize a person, we do not have much time, so we need to know the minimum state where we throw the subject to accept each of the following suggestions:

_A._   *Z1. (We tip) Every night when you lie on your bed, you will feel very relaxed, more relaxed, and want to sleep, because the only way you can rest and prepare for the next day ... Z1*

_B._   *Z1. (We tip) Whenever you sit down to study, you will feel very relaxed, and see how well you assimilate every page you read, memorize Z1 will cost less ...*

_C._   *Z2. (We give an order. Sleeping) Every night when you lie on your bed, you'll see how you fall into a deep sleep. There will be nothing to be concerned about. Although try to stay awake, your eyes will close and you can rest peacefully that night Z2 ...*

6)   Write the suggestions you could say the Z1 and Z2 been a person who wants to stop being afraid of cats:

For the Z1: *You know you're scared cats for no reason? Just realize that almost nobody is afraid of cats. Why is that? Surely, because cats do nothing. They are only small pets that give affection to their owners. (Everything that looks like a council of why cats do nothing, is correct.)*

FOR EXAMPLE:
_Z1:_ *From now, you'll feel more and more security and more and more confident when facing a cat, from now you will see how begin to have value against cats, and you will feel less and less fear of cats to the point of starting to feel more and more relaxed when facing one.*

For Z2: *From now on cats do not get scared. You understand that your fear is not based on anything and like all people, to you also like cats. (We took advantage that we can give orders and directly apply them as directly as saying. "From now on cats do not get scared.")*

FOR EXAMPLE:
_Z2:_ *From now, you feel more and more security and more and more confident when facing a pleasing, the degree of great courage and courage, confidence and security that allow you to never be afraid of cats, from now you will see how you begin to have more and more love and sympathy against the cat's degree never again feel negative feelings and emotions to the point you begin to feel more and more calm, in peace and in control by contact with one.*

CHAPTER THREE: THE TWO (2) MESMER RESOURCES AND TOOLS

Apprentice; all professional hypnotist, has two (2) useful resources and tools used throughout his hypnotic act, either at its Therapeutics Clinical Hypnosis, or its Hypnosis Shows Street or Show. These are useful resources: Fascination and Suggestion.

The first tool: FASCINATION

All human beings, have visual perception, auditory perception, kinesthetic sensory perception and perception (smell and taste). These perceptions, they are also known in other fields and disciplines such as sub modalities. The representative Sub modalities or perceptual systems applied to hypnosis, are the different variables that belong to the same access perception we use "{Externally to perceive the world}" - e "{Internally shaped to represent experience}". And that define the difference in how we process, store and encode different hypnotic phenomena and processes we are experiencing through the "different sensory channels" (VAK- "O and G"). Visual what we see, what we hear auditory, kinesthetic we touch and feel,

Now to continue with the subject of fascination. Imagine my apprentice, that our consciousness or conscious mind is an analyzer, which likes to analyze everything (the what, the why, the what, when, how and where ...) That consciousness or conscious mind has a kind of filter information, call CRITICAL FACTOR of MIND. This critical factor is who determines what matters and what does not; Similarly, one who determines what comes into our subconscious mind and what is rejected. In other words, the critical factor is not interested in what it rejects.

I will illustrate this idea with a GOOD EXAMPLE: Suppose that the hypnotist gives suggestions to a person, your hand will not be able to take off his forehead. Then the consciousness of the subject is active and the critical factor acts and thinks ... "How my hand will not be able to take off my forehead? If you are well outside hypnosis ... That order cannot be fulfilled ... "That's when all our suggestions are rejected without giving effect.

The good news apprentice; is; our consciousness or conscious mind can only analyze a perception element at a time, either (visual, auditory, kinesthetic or sensory). Let me give you another example: Imagine you're in college, attending the class teacher. With our attentive consciousness to what the teacher says, suddenly someone comes unannounced through the door ... At that moment, the door opened we are not attentive to the teacher (logically) because our "consciousness swerved to see" (who he is coming in the door).

Well, in HYPNOSIS advantage of those moments of distraction critical to embed the order directly into the subconscious mind of the person. Style and compass describing mental images generated in the patient or participant a sense of deepening the state we want to induce. Or the combination of several of these elements simultaneously hypnotic fascination.

IN SUMMARY: Fascination, is to keep the critical and conscious mind of the subject occupied, to embed suggestions (orders), and that these are more easily processed by the subconscious of the person.

Apprentice, to apply these techniques correctly Alluring surely orders, suggestions and inductions will not be the critical factor of the mind analyzed; and for that reason, they will be instantly more easily assimilated by the subconscious of the person. AND READY Already get the picture, right? Alluring the two techniques bind, and then the brain through the instructions of the hypnotist does all the work. ¿Interesting right?

The second tool: SUGGESTION

We have just seen that when the hypnotist fascinates the subject by combining visual perceptions, auditory, kinesthetic and sensory also uses suggestion "{(Order covert)}" with all its language both verbal and non-verbal (body posture "look, gestures", "Symmetry" - "Orientation" - "Tilt" - "cocked" and "Micro-Facial Expressions") to generate a subliminal and subjective order that will allow us to access the subconscious mind and the unconscious of the person. In other words, my apprentice, suggestion, are "covert orders" generated through verbal and nonverbal language in a subtle way, that distracts the critical factor of the mind and allows us to embed commands to the subconscious so that it accepts them more easily.

What role played by language (verbal and non-verbal) in the process of suggestion "creation of covert orders" on deepening orders in the unconscious? When the hypnotist speaks and expresses itself, seeks to generate RAPPORT and use linguistic and bodily structures as symmetrically as possible to mental and psychological structures of the subject, thus allowing pacing and create an illusion of mirroring in order to establish a better rapport with the people with whom we are working, thus facilitating ease the introduction of suggestion "creation of covert orders" in the hypnotic process. Thus, both the words, phrases, sentences, look, gestures will find less resistance and more rapidly assimilated by the unconscious and the subconscious mind subject.

IN SUMMARY: The suggestion, are "embedded commands" or "covert orders" generated through the fascination in conjunction with verbal and nonverbal in a subtle way, so that the unconscious and the subconscious mind of the person accepts suggestions (orders) more easily.

EXERCISES

1.-Name the two (2) tools or resources of a good hypnotist. And Explain briefly what each one of them, explain in their own words (be brief) and some examples?
R) =

2.- WHAT IS THE MOST IMPORTANT THING YOU HAVE LEARNED IN THIS LESSON?
R) =

Good **LEARNERS**, we have **Ended with the Third Chapter**! Again, very lucky with the exercises. Remember if you have any questions to answer the questionnaire *(The answers are available on the next page)* You've come a long way, congratulations ... I hope you're learning a lot "And it's just the beginning of your training in this great hypnotic art" "*If you have any questions, you can "email me directly to my mail (E-mail)*".

MásterCoach.YlichTarazona@gmail.com
http://www.reingenieriamentalconpnl.com

Congratulations "**LEARNERS** "For having come to this part of the book; I'm glad, to be your mentor and master teacher in this great art of hypnosis. The final test of the book "The power of hypnosis" will you have learned to fully master the techniques and methodologies most powerful and effective to generate a state of Trance Hypnotic led by hypnosis.

(I'll share more information with you, below) I mention something very personal, you know me personally, I love teaching hypnosis is one of my greatest passions. But do and to perform all the extraordinary things that can be achieved through hypnosis, as are lucid dreams, astral travel, body experiences and hypnotic phenomena among other things. Which at first may seem like something difficult, complicated or even incredible; well yes, it is true, a little, but only at the beginning here =) "We know that home is." But I assure you, that you too can master this hypnotic art completely, because I think teach you how, and when you start to live your own experiences will be very curious and interesting for you, you'll see ^ _ ^ Well I hope soon to have your own news.

If you enjoyed this workshop hypnosis, and want to "help" with your contribution, to support me to continue doing this wonderful work, which, with love, prepared for you. You can do this through the following link.

http://bit.ly/PaypalDonación
Thank you for your contribution

"Success is not a one-day event, it is a lifelong process is repeated. You can be a winner in his life if he tries. BECAUSE YOU ARE A WINNER born and from the moment of conception ... Remember: Successful people engage in activities that allow them to win from time to time; because they know that both the triumph, victory and conquest are habits that should constantly develop in their lifestyle ... Successful people; Also, they keep in mind that it is also losing wins. Because they know that every failure brings them closer to their purpose and that every defeat strengthens and teaches them what to improve. In After; both triumphs and defeats, are so important for success, that when we learn from them we become stronger and worthy of living that style and extraordinary quality of life for which we have both strive day after day. "- YLICH TARAZONA. -

SOLUTIONS exercise Lesson Previous:

SHORT ANSWER:

1. Fascination, is to keep the critical factor of the conscious mind and occupied subject to embed suggestions, and these are more easily processed by the subconscious of the person.

2. Suggestion, they are "embedded commands" generated by the fascination together with verbal and non-verbal language in a subtle way, so that the unconscious and the subconscious mind of the person accepts orders more easily.

LONG ANSWER:

1) **FASCINATION** as a tool used in hypnosis, is the resource that allows us to try to divert the critical factor of consciousness of the subject in order to implement the suggestion (covert orders) directly into the subconscious mind of the person through various techniques of Visual Perception, auditory, kinesthetic or *sensory* so that suggestions (covert orders) are more easily processed by the unconscious of the subject.

2) **SUGGESTION** is "{(Order Covert)}" that next to both verbal and nonverbal (**BODY POSTURE** *"Look, gestures"*, *"Symmetry"* - *"Orientation"* - *"Tilt"* - *"cocked" and "Micro-Facial Expressions")* They allow us to generate subliminal and subjective orders entitling us access to the subconscious mind and the unconscious of the person. In other words, suggestion, are "covert orders" generated through verbal and nonverbal language in a subtle way, that distracts the critical factor of the mind and allows us to embed commands to the subconscious so that it accepts them more easily.

WHAT IS THE MOST IMPORTANT THING YOU HAVE LEARNED IN THIS LESSON?
R) = "Free Reply" Each participant may have to answer this question as you have learned and what they would like to share with the facilitator.

If you enjoyed this workshop hypnosis, and want to "help" with your contribution, to support me to continue doing this wonderful work, which, with love, prepared for you. You can do this through the following link.

---

http://bit.ly/PaypalDonación
Thank you for your contribution

CHAPTER FOURTH: HYPNOSIS TECHNIQUES "MESMER TOOLS" According to the teachings of ERIC BARONE and JACQUES MANDORLA

Hello such APPRENTICES; a great greeting for everyone s. Welcome to the fourth part of this course practice hypnosis! In this chapter we will learn to create our own hypnosis techniques. I'll opt for the classification and explanation given us Eric Barone and Jacques Mandorla in his book ABC of Hypnosis (Develop Your Mental Potential) of editorial Tikal. All these teachings that I will share with you below are adapted from the book. Well; because I found excellent and very interesting work. So, all that "great families of Hypnosis the Eight" appears in the sections of an adaptation to design to create this part of the book "{[Eric Barone and Jacques Mandorla in his ABC of Hypnosis (Develop your Mental) potential editorial Tikal]} ".

Eight Great Families of Hypnosis

SENSORY Family

This family includes all sensory techniques using procedures such as (technique *eye fixation* mainly proposals *James Braid*). rotating spirals are considered part of these techniques the well-known ("hypnotics disks") the *("Pendulums")*, The ("lights or strobe lights"), the ("color fringes") among others.

Apprentice; in this technique Sensory FAMILY, it should take into account the auditory perceptions "MUSIC" (background or musical prelude), "tone" (rhythm, style and rhythm) as well as all regular or irregular beeps. Similarly; all tactile perceptions (Kinesthetic physical contact), "Non-verbal language" can also be used (*body posture*, *Look, mannerisms, gestures, facial micro-expressions)* among others. Because all these procedures, our eyes look different techniques actually obey the following strategy **SENSORY FAMILY** (Let's see how these methods synergistically, holistic and comprehensive work) ...

1. Create a situation in which we know the psychological consequences.

2. Sync through suggestion.

3. Divert suggestion towards a certain goal.

Take an example of this strategy:

Strategy "Phraseology"

Create a situation in which the psychological consequences are known.	*"Now I place a point before your eyes and you will follow him in all his movements; that point swivels from left to right, right to left, follow that point permanently … "*
Sync through suggestion.	*"As follows that point swivels, you feel your eyes get tired increasingly, their eyelids become heavy, more and more heavy and tired. Close progressively they are become so heavy that it can no longer keep my eyes open, heavy and tired. Feel like sleeping; more and more heavy and tired, more and more you feel like sleeping … "*
Divert suggestion towards the objective.	*"His eyelids close more and more, and the more you close more deeply into sleep. His body falls more and more into a deep sleep … "*

Let's explain a bit:

1.   CREATE A SITUATION IN WHICH THE KNOWN psychological consequences.

When we put a point before the eyes of a subject and make it swing, we know that certain weariness appears. **If what is placed before the subject are colored stripes, we know that the colors tend to blend (optical effect). If a stationary coil is placed, we know that the subject will soon have the impression that the spiral will spin.** Already you understand the idea?

TRICK As you see, we try to create a situation in which we know the consequences, and then attribute these consequences to which you want to sleep. (Actually, there is no relationship, but we must make him believe that if any)

FOR EXAMPLE: In the test fall back, we know that when someone is late with feet together or later will falter. If we say we will first stagger, and staggers; when you say you will start to fall back It will fall back! Do you see how easy it is? …

2.   SYNCHRONIZE THROUGH THE SUGGESTION.

The suggestion of the hypnotist can make believe the individual that he (hypnotist) has produced the same effect.

It is therefore claim that hypnotic phenomenon in our favor; which, however, he would have produced. The suggestion of the hypnotist is to persuade the subject that the hypnotic phenomenon is due to him (hypnotist). At that time, the unconscious of the subject will give the hypnotist does not actually own power; only it thought so. That does not mean that the hypnotist allows only has the power that the individual grants and grant wishes.

3.   DIVERT THE SUGGESTION.

If you managed to get the individual to accept a fact, however, would have occurred spontaneously or naturally (synchronized by means of suggestion), that individual is ready to accept a slight deviation thanks to the power that has given us unconsciously. If, feeling tired, you have agreed to close their eyes, convinced that I am the author of his weariness, much more so accept, relax and sleep soundly.

The ability of the hypnotist will be to progress smoothly towards increasingly nearby states, and not spend too abruptly things away. It is normal to ask someone to sleep after closing your eyes and have relaxed; abnormal would ask that his whole body contracted after closing the eyes. Already you understand the idea, right?

Therefore, hypnosis (hypnotic process) will progress through very staggered phases. They have invented hundreds of alleged techniques or techniques, but when we see a hypnotist on stage with eyes wide open, staring at someone, is mainly using this technique. In this SENSORIAL family; thousands of procedures are collected, and you my dear apprentice, you must memorize all these strategies.

THAT IS TO SAY:
1.   Create a situation in which we know the psychological consequences.
2.   Sync through suggestion.
3.   Divert suggestion towards a certain goal.

Invent Your Techniques:

Replaces the light from an object point, vision sound, etc.

You've just mastered a strategy, you can create on your own new techniques, and that my dear apprentice, it is what I want you to learn to develop.

Under no circumstances should leave a random detail; at all times you must know where you are if you want to know where to go. (You must know what strategy you are and when you should move to the next.) It's all about experience.

> *In the same way that a driver is responsible for his vehicle from the moment he gets going, your apprentice, you become responsible for the conduct of hypnosis from the moment the start.*
>
> *You must not betray the trust that an individual has placed in you when subjected to a hypnosis session. It is your responsibility to correct what you have to do, in the manner and in the appropriate manner.*

EXERCISE:

1.- You have to create and innovate a technique of this family (SENSORY). Note the many suggestions I've given you in this chapter. (There is no answer for this exercise) all I'll leave to your imagination, creativity and intuition. I know you can do it, I believe in you my apprentice.

("Advance Directives Before performing the exercise")

To perform this exercise; I propose to the induction technique or "test Suggestibility" known as the Crash Test back, which is one of the most efficient and effective to begin producing hypnotic phenomena with 90% chance of success techniques ... Now you TEST fails FALL BACK in writing later.

First of all, invite a person of trust, someone you trust, and yet that person also trust you. To make your first induction.

FIRST: You have to clarify, it's just an experiment, that at no time enter under hypnosis. And at no time slumber, will not run any risk of getting hurt by falling back since the consciously react to steady herself. Let him know that you'll be there to support him at all times, that you're no alert, ready and attentive to properly hold.

Tell him to put his feet together, to relax, to let all your muscles relaxed, to concentrate on your breathing. Put yourself behind the subject, put your hands 2 or 3 feet away from him, and begins with hypnotic suggestion.

> **IMPORTANT** *Although you told him the person who, if he feels he is going to fall, to stay calm and relaxed, because you'll be there, alert and caring for him at all times and at every step of the procedure. Remember to be careful if you / the need to take so you will not fall. That's why I like to explain it clearer that, if he sees that falls backward, to react, to open your eyes, and you step back and you're done you seen how easy it is? So, apprentice is in you achieving this your first challenge ... I'll be quiet here with you, always in every step. Just follow my instructions and recommendations. And you'll see how everything will be fine ...*

> *If you see your suggestions and hypnotic inductions do not work, try changing the tone of voice and your body posture, as we saw in the previous chapter. And above all, take advantage of every little move the person to do, to make him believe that from this movement that has already occurred will feel it falls back. AND READY ... It's APPRENTICE, and started your first steps on your way to becoming the hypnotist I know you and you will become.*

Then I let the technique of falling backwards. Where I explain step by step, as you must do, and that recommendations have to take leave for the technique correctly, so can these quiet and relax ^ _ ^.

Suggestibility test "Crash Test BACK" Example and Explanation

(The following is a test of suggestibility that is the subject to hypnotize, to check the degree of hyper-suggestibility and answer before the suggestions and hypnotic inductions ... This test; It is unfinished, so you know apprentice you have to do, use your intuition, your imagination and creativity; and end it with your own words ...)

But before proceeding teach you a powerful tool magnetism, called MOPPAO which is useful in testing fall back.

Magnetism tool: MOPPAO

It refers to magnetism, developed and popularized by Franz Anton Mesmer's theory of "Animal Magnetism" later called *MESMERISM which it is related to magnetic fields or energy field.*

The interesting thing about this tool Magnetism: MOPPAO is that when a hypnotist places his hands about four (4) to five (5) centimeters of certain vital points of the individual, can cause drowsiness and a sense of transfer of magnetism from the hypnotist to the hypnotized. The **Magnetic fields**, Or Energy Field Vital Points (also known as *chakras)* They are large concentrations of energy channels in nerves and all humans.

According to the theory of Chakras, as these energy fields act in the 4 most important vital points in hypnosis.

Front: The two outstretched hands
Of the throat: The two outstretched hands
Of the heart: The right hand extended
Part of the navel: The right hand extended

EXERCISE: PROOF FALL BACK

"The hypnotist is placed behind the person (Place the subject with feet together, eyes closed and body relaxed). Once; standing both together, the hypnotist puts his hands on the shoulders of the subject to 4 or 5 centimeters without touching the person "or" places one of his hands in front of the person at the height of the solar plexus (chest) and the other hand placed behind the subject in the back at the same height each other about 4 or 5 centimeters without touching the person (technical MOPPAO). Once hands positioned at the position; without touching him, (While you hypnotist focuses on the image of the subject falling backward, as if Jan is already happening moment) you say:

From now begin to feel a very strange feeling, you feel like your body slowly begins to move gently back and forth, you feel like those little movements are increasing more and more, you feel like a strange force will begin balance forward and backward. That's right, you're doing great, perfect and you started wobble...

(Continue it you, six to seven lines).

CURIOUS EXERCISE Once you have completed writing and complete the exercise test fall back upon completion you can implement it with someone in which you have confidence. "The biggest challenge brake or technique, by the subject who was going to influence, is the fear of falling to the ground". (To fix this, it is very simple, just enough to explain to the person that is not going to sleep, which is always awake, attentive and alert throughout the hypnotic procedure). "It is important to let the person know that when you feel it will now fall back to get carried away, we'll be there waiting on him that all is well, that we at all times be alert to exercise out properly and to hold at all times".

Apprentice important to you. You not necessarily have to learning you text or caletre memory, it's just important learning you the basic steps, follow an order, stay focused on the target and follow the steps, but using your own words. It will simply try to convince the subconscious of the subject is falling, and seize any rocking motion of his body, indicating that they have already begun effects See how easy it is? ". TIP: If you do not give the result to the first, quiet, okay, relax and try again. But this time try to go changing the tone, volume and rhythm of the voice until you find one that works. (This test poses no danger, because it is completely safe. The only precaution you must take is to explain to the subject when you see is falling back, react and place the foot.)

Good **LEARNERS**, we have **Completed this first lesson of the fourth chapter**! As always, I wish you luck with the exercises.

Remember, if you have any questions to perform the exercise correctly, *(You know you can count on me for anything you need. - The Complete test, find next page)* and in some subsequent chapters more hasten; I'll share more elements, so that the fences incorporating the test as fences gaining experience.

I know that this exercise is a higher level, but you are here to learn, so I just invite you to take action and make things happen, I believe in you, and I know you can achieve. Remember that "If you have any questions, you can "directly write to my mail (E-mail)".

MásterCoach.YlichTarazona@gmail.com
http://www.reingenieriamentalconpnl.com

Apprentice than good, I am very glad and You've come a long way, I hope you'll be liking the HYPNOSIS COURSE PRACTICE. And above all you're learning a lot; and that the realization of this exercise (Test Suggestibility) of the Fall Backwards Sensory Family, carry "Your Knowledge and Skills Hypnotic the Next Level".

Well, I hope to read your messages from the "Comments" section of my website Oh! APPRENTICE, I would also like you to comment me the experience you had when testing suggestibility fall back. Bye- I hope to have news soon yours ... ^ _ ^!

If you enjoyed this workshop hypnosis, and want to "help" with your contribution, to support me to continue doing this wonderful work, which, with love, prepared for you. You can do this through the following link.

---

http://bit.ly/PaypalDonación
Thank you for your contribution

WHAT distinguishes the winners from the losers? "Winners are concentrated at all times what they know they can do well, talents, strengths, skills, abilities and skills. Although they recognize they have weaknesses; They never focus on them, but working on them ... while the losers are scattered thinking about all those things when they do not want to do evil; focusing on their weaknesses, limitations and lack of talent, but they know they have strengths, never seems to realize them ... If you're good at persuading, influencing or hypnotizing, then focus on those potentialities and weaknesses will become stronger as you work on them slowly, without leaving aside those things where you know you're really good ... Here lies the big difference that makes the difference between winners and losers, how to act before adversity. "- YLICH TARAZONA. -

As promised, here's apprentice everything you need to know to perform effectively
TEST FALL BACK correctly

Suggestibility test "TEST FALL BACK" Complete Application Tool:

"The hypnotist is placed behind the person (Place the subject with feet together, eyes closed and body relaxed). Once; standing both together, the hypnotist puts his hands on the shoulders of the subject to 4 or 5 centimeters without touching the person "or" places one of his hands in front of the person at the height of the solar plexus (chest) and the other hand placed behind the subject in the back at the same height each other about 4 or 5 centimeters without touching the person (technical MOPPAO). Once hands positioned at the position; without touching him, (While you hypnotist focuses on the image of the subject falling backward, as if Jan is already happening moment) you say:

From the moment I want you to focus on your whole body, just now begin to feel a very strange feeling, soon, you'll notice that your body sways and feel like your body slowly begins to move smoothly forward and back, you feel like those little movements are increasing more and more, you feel like an alien force balance begin gently forward and backward. And I want you when you start to feel that sense of swing, you focus on the experience you are living and experiencing your body and feel that strange force begins to move and balance your body. " That's right, you're doing very well, and started to wobble perfect. Hereinafter, begin to notice how your body feels strongly becoming more and more pushed and drawn back, the feeling is so very real, you can no longer resist; and decide to give, you decide to get carried away by that feeling so, right... You're doing fine, "See, you felt that? Your body has moved ... From now on, the strange force takes control of your body, and begins gently wobble more and more and push you forward and backward. You cannot go longer standing. That strange feeling of wellbeing is stronger than you. The movements are becoming more and more intense, and you may notice the right? You're doing fine, right. Now feels like those little movements are increasing more and more, you cannot stop them, it is impossible to keep still,

(Continues until fall. The normal for a person to fall time are 2, 3 and 5 minutes) (Warning! ... There are also people who fall at 10 and 30 seconds! So, all times have to be alert, ready and able to hold on time and prevent them from going to fall.)

This test of suggestibility always works 90% of the time, with high probability of success, if we are careful and pay attention to any movement that makes the person, and make him believe, feel and experience in the subject's mind that this movement has been infused by that strange force.

Since I have made the full text of suggestibility TEST FALL BACK, I study it, practice, repeat it in your mind several times about learning you order and the fundamental steps. Once you've done it already. Ready, forget about it, is only a guide to help you get started. Better you learn the basic steps, order and basic ideas and then you get an idea of what you have to say in your own words, instead of trying to learning you text memory. You have to be yourself able to invent an almost equal or similar, which I just I have proposed, then you with your imagination, creativity and intuition to adapt to your own style and ready apprentice, you've mastered the first TASTE OF suggestibility this workshop.

My dear apprentice, in the seventh, back to share you more items, tips and resources for incorporating fences Test Fall Backwards as fences gaining more and more experience ^ _ ^

Well apprentice, remember that hope to read your messages from the "Comments" section of my website or directly from my E-mail. Ah! APPRENTICE, one more thing, I also want you to comment me as I was on the experience you had when testing suggestibility fall back. See you soon for now- I hope to have news of you my great friends (as) ... ^ _ ^!

MásterCoach.YlichTarazona@gmail.com
http://www.reingenieriamentalconpnl.com

If you enjoyed this workshop hypnosis, and want to "help" with your contribution, to support me to continue doing this wonderful work, which, with love, prepared for you. You can do this through the following link.

---

http://bit.ly/PaypalDonación
Thank you for your contribution

"Dreams are like an energy source. It is what motivates us and drives us to go beyond our limitations. It is the burning desire to achieve what we all desire to conquer. Is so powerful and so great that when part of ourselves we are inspired to take action. It's what he does; we continue forward, when our mind tells us we cannot anymore. It is what makes us go the extru kilometer. Is; the end of the day, the reason for our existence "
-. YLICH TARAZONA. -

Two new types of hypnosis techniques

Hello such apprentice; a great greeting for everyone in this new lesson will continue to learn two new types more than hypnosis techniques of "Big Eight Families of Hypnosis" techniques that are studying the book "{[Eric Barone and Jacques Mandorla in his ABC Hypnosis (Build your Mental Potential) of Editorial Tikal]} ". The development of this lesson; it will be similar to the previous section. See the description of the technique, we will share some examples and references to understand the main idea. And then at the end of the exercise section, you will have the task, create, innovate and design a new technique of hypnosis for each family to see. Before we begin, I want to thank all the interest you're putting into this course of practice hypnosis. XD you're doing super; so, congratulations apprentice, and continue with your lessons. So, without further ado let's begin.

2. Family PHYSIOLOGICAL

For this second family in particular, must take special care. It is the only one that should not be used before first master correctly. For the development of this family, first it is recommended to properly meet its possible contraindications, such as. (Wording of example we could use a person suffering from heart problems, heart problems or problems of high blood pressure "... Little notes like the heart decreases your heart rate ... ") the typical strategy of this family is as follows:

Strategy Phraseology

Cause a physiological action from which a time separation occurs.	*Now I put my thumbs on your eyelids closed, gently support without you no harm, and I'll give you a gentle massage in the eye. Gradually, you'll notice as the heart decreases your heart rate and you will fall in a wonderful state of peace, tranquility and relaxation ...*
Use the supposed separation to introduce a suggestion of depth.	*And now, you slip away, sleeping more and more deeply, you slip deeper into a hypnotic sleep ...*

We will analyze this strategy:

Although we believe that we control perfectly into our daily lives, it is very normal for a surprise, an accident, something unusual, causing a kind of interruption of control, that consciousness has on our body.

__FOR EXAMPLE__: A violent surprise, a brutal accident, a very loud noise can provoke an emotion, which may be accompanied by heart acceleration, sudden sweating and even a start. "This moment can be called separation." (This is a very brief suspension control our body by our consciousness). Mesmer, knowing this action and use it to your advantage, voluntarily cause certain separations. But having very little control over the subject, will assume some of those moments, or agree with him beforehand, a signal that allows to detect them better.

To continue the previous example: If we make a light massage of the eyeballs; about three (3) minutes long, a simple physiological reflex will decrease the heart rate of the subject. The suggestion will be oriented in the direction of synchronization: "[Suggest the individual phenomenon known generally happens three minutes (decreased heart rate), and introduce a suggestion (deep sleep) to associate with the separation]". Separation (decrease heart rate) is then a kind of gap directly open to the unconscious person. The suggestion is entered (deep sleep) then approach the unconscious much faster and "induced hypnotic phenomenon created".

__RECOMMENDATION__ This technique is absolutely inadvisable to all those who use contact lenses (lenses - eyeglasses) or suffering from cardiac disorders.

EXAMPLES:

Place one finger on the center front of the subject; "Where it is located (The Third Eye)". Ask the subject to imagine that his forehead is transparent; translucent. And you can follow and focus on the finger is at the center of his forehead; and then a light finger pressure to the front and remove it several times, telling the person to focus on looking at the finger approaches and moves away from the center of his forehead.

And from a number of attempts, 3 for example. The separation is likely to occur when the eye revulsion is maximized.

This technique does not imply any danger, nor has any contraindications. Sometimes, resulting in some subjects, it is to provoke a reflection sleep.

At certain stages of REM sleep our eyes are blank; facing the front center of the mind. The fact recreates this natural, artificially state can cause a phenomenon of feedback (remember) sleep.

Another technique that can be used is hyperventilation, which is riskier than inflating a rubber mat blowing (Inflating an inflatable mattress). It is the individual "Inhale (aspire) and Exhale (breathe out) to Inhale (vacuum) and Exhale (breathe out) increasingly rapid, rapid and deep. Increasing the amount of oxygen in the blood will cause a slight dizziness. You can agree with the person a specific signal indicating at what point we begin to feel it. This (vertigo), is a characteristic separation; the suggestion (sleep) that is introduced during the period in which the subject experiences it. And ready to do the technique correctly suggestion will be worked, and the subject will feel the sensation (suggestion of sleep) and our partner unconsciously. That is to say,

RECOMMENDATION: *There should practice this technique hyperventilation people with tetanic trends or spasmophilia or suffer disturbances or respiratory conditions (syndrome that regroups several symptoms related to state anxiety sometimes expressed with breathtaking crisis.).*

In order to fully exploit the hypnotic processes (get more out of hypnosis) always need the consent of the subject unconscious. The fact that a person indicates us his conscious and voluntary agreement agrees to be hypnotized by us, does not necessarily mean that your unconscious agrees. While the hypnotic state depends on its consent competition, maximum use of hypnosis may be used only from a profound agreement with the unconscious and the subconscious mind of the subject.

3. The Family PSICOIMAGINARIA

This third family is less risky than the previous one, but it requires more competition verbal (speaking ability) by the hypnotist.

With regard to this third family, the hypnotist must transfer a progressive relaxation of the body and mind of the subject, tending a progressive lowering of consciousness. As, for example, with the "Technical De La Barca" or any other technique that produces feeling of mobility. In the case of the technique or concept of a boat; this is moving in the ocean, and we can compare it to mind allegorically shows that sails to the deep sea (which would sail or dive into the depths of their minds). This technique can also be used with any other action that represents movement or mobility. As it might be down the stairs, and as each step down, deeper and deeper comes into hypnotic trance. Another example might be, Descend lift. And as the elevator goes down each floor or level, and your mind is descending deeper and deeper into a deep sleep. Already you got the idea, right? That's apprentice. Congratulations, you now taking these concepts in mind, we continue to learn more about this family in particular to clarify further on the subject.

Presenting a mobile concept (constant motion - having mobility) in the Family PSICOIMAGINARIA has the advantage of creating a sense escalation in the subject, in his own relaxation, both mental and physical. This allows us to take advantage of this progressive feeling of deep relaxation to help the person experiencing the desired hypnotic phenomenon.

EXPLANATION: The decrease in consciousness is symbolized allegorically and metaphorically, such as: The entrance of the boat in the mountains or deep in the ocean at sunset. The decrease in brightness equivalent to the progressive disappearance of consciousness and vigilance of the subject. In the case of the stairs, the act of lowering each step of it represents a drop or decrease in our consciousness the desired hypnotic state. The same applies to the elevator, the elevator down image down each floor or level, represents the subject's ability to move up or down more hypnotic trance. In all three cases; THE PURPOSE IS TO CREATE A FEELING OF RELAXATION PROGRESSIVE, ALLOWING THE SUBJECT ENTER INTO HYPNOSIS, ie, in the state of deep sleep that people go into hypnosis metaphorically

---

These images are very rich in information. What better indicate the success of these techniques of suggestion, is both visual and imaginative capacity of the subject, which must be extremely creative; and the expressive power of verbal recall and intuitive, imaginative and creative ability of the hypnotist, to stimulate multisensory sensations in the subject, and the mobilization of thoughts, emotions, memories and creative imagination of the hypnotized.

As you see, is the same family Technical PSICOIMAGINARIA only that the ship navigates the ocean, can be replaced by a lift floor to floor or level slips level down, or an escalator descending step by and step down to reach the levels below.

IMPORTANT *When the hypnotist through CALIBRATION is, (observation technique) have the impression that the subject reaches a loss of consciousness, you should immediately introduce a suggestion of depth, with has the subject to prolong and deepen the desired state.*

Strategy Phraseology

Create an imaginary situation whose natural development is symmetrical and similar with regard to the physiological states through which must pass the subject in question.	*Imagine your body lying in a boat, perfectly relaxed. That boat floats gently and glides slowly, more and softer and quietly. As the boat glides and sails the vast ocean, your body relaxes progressively more and more in that state of deep sleep ...*
Agreeing a sign or a signal to detect separation (in this case, relaxation of the muscles of the legs. But the sign also could lower the index finger, which had been suspended, just one stop seeing and thinking, that is, from the entry into the cave.)	*You slip quietly. The river flows near a mountain. It is about more and more. Your body relaxes more and more deeply. Feel deep peace, quiet relaxation, calmness and serenity. At the foot of the mountain, the river enters a cave.* *As your boat approaches the grotto, you slip more and more into a state of tranquility and peace. The boat gets closer and closer to the grotto. This cave is dark, but quiet, serene and*

	safe. The boat slowly enters the grotto. Light decreases gradually increasing. Your body relaxes more and more too, outshines you more and more this feeling perfectly rested, calm, relaxed in peace and quiet, with a feeling I will sleep ...
Deepen the state created.	You are asleep! Sleep NOW

APPRENTICE good, for now we have only one more family to teach in this course and to practice hypnosis. (Actually, there are many more families, but they are very complicated techniques I just use these families. But I know that I've taught so far, including me, has done very well) Teaching these four families here I think that simplified the course pretty well, making it shorter, easy and convenient for you who are starting in this wonderful art of hypnosis. But I promise that at the end of the fourth chapter, when we studied all four families, teach them one (1) variation of hypnosis techniques PSICOCONFLICTIVA family study later in the next lesson. This change will allow them to perform "Fast Hypnosis Advanced Techniques" to anyone. Interesting ¿truth? Well this will be my gift to you What do you think? Okay, then let's continue.

EXERCISES:

Create, write and design the wording of hypnosis technique belonging to each of the two families who have studied in this lesson. That is, a technique of physiological family and another family of psicoimaginaria. (To see how this our creativity ...) (XD Apprentice, no solution for this exercise.); so is your time to take action, make things happen and show your ingenuity, creativity, intuition and desire to become one of the best hypnotists. So, go ahead, I know you can, I believe in you, in your potential and your ability to perform these two exercises I propose. APPRENTICE So, go ahead and get to work.

XD apprentice, but it's up to you! So far, they have done extremely well. And I know you will continue to improve, you and I together, we will achieve great things with hypnosis. I'm giving my best for you, now you put the best they can give and I know you will go far.

Wuao **LEARNERS** As time passes and We have **reached the second part of this lesson**! As always, I wish you every success with the exercise. These exercises have no answers or solutions, since the idea is to activate your creativity and ingenuity. But remember that if you have any questions to answer the questionnaire *(You know you can always count on me, for what you need)* I hope you're learning a lot, and that these two families, physiological and psicoimaginaria, with "Your talents Hypnotics to Next Level"

Remember that "*If you have any questions, you can "email me directly to my mail (E-mail)*". **Again,** many thanks apprentice; for your interest you have shown in this hypnosis course practice. I'll be happy to answer your questions, comments and ideas.

GOOD NEWS APPRENTICE... I think in about three (3) to four (4) chapters, just the essence of this course of practice hypnosis. =)
So, go to the next chapter! XD ^ _ ^

MásterCoach.YlichTarazona@gmail.com
http://www.reingenieriamentalconpnl.com

If you enjoyed this workshop hypnosis, and want to "help" with your contribution, to support me to continue doing this wonderful work, which, with love, prepared for you. You can do this through the following link.

http://bit.ly/PaypalDonación
Thank you for your contribution

THE POWER OF ACTION PERFORMANCE AND FOCUS *"Among older are your efforts and constant dedication to a preset goal ahead and planning. The better the results and achievements. "- YLICH TARAZONA. -*

FAMILY FOURTH HYPNOSIS TECHNIQUES

Hello such apprentice; a great greeting for everyone s, have reached the end of this lesson hypnosis techniques, today we will learn the fourth and last of the families of "Big Eight Families of Hypnosis" techniques that are studying the book "{[Eric Barone and Jacques Mandorla in his ABC of Hypnosis (Develop your Mental Potential) of Editions Tikal]} ". The development of this lesson; It will be similar to the last preceding paragraphs. See the description of the technique, we will share some examples and references to understand the main idea. And then at the end of the exercise section, you will have the task, create, innovate and design a new technique of hypnosis for the last fourth family discussed in this course of practice hypnosis.

Before starting apprentice, I want to thank you all, for the interest you have been giving to this wonderful course of practical hypnosis, that with much love and summarized and prepared for you. I have received up to 80 emails a day! Wuao; In truth, I will try to answer all of you in due course, my dear apprentices. For now; without further delay, we begin...

4. Family PSICOCONFLICTIVA. "Suggestibility test"

Apprentice, this fourth family of hypnosis techniques, has a high degree of difficulty for the hypnotist. And requiring greater strength, confidence and authority, along with a verbal fluency. Based on the charisma, the sheer force of suggestion or positive influence of the hypnotist into the subject. PSICOCONFLICTIVA THIS FAMILY IS USED AS PROOF OF suggestibility. It is challenging to master this method, since it requires to make decisions quickly to unanticipated challenges. Remember the success of this family when putting it into practice will depend directly and exclusively of his conviction.

Strategy (What is in bold)
Phraseology (What is italicized)

Create a situation "Suggestibility test" with two possible outputs.

Stretching out his right arm forward and upward with fists, now your arm becomes more and more rigid, becomes like a stick of solid, rigid and immobile steel, more and more solid, rigid and immobile until the point you're trying to bend and bend YOU CAN NOT ALREADY.

Closes, the stronger left hand you can, more and stronger, more and more tight, now your hand is made of cast steel, solid very closed, is so close that you try to open it and YOU CAN NO LONGER open.

When we launched the challenge "Stiff Arm or Closed Fist."

1. From now on, your arm is so stiff, you can no longer bend.
2. From now on, your fist is so closed, you can no longer open.

(With these two (2) challenges, we can find two (2) possible behaviors)

Case 1 A. If the arm challenge will fail, to regain control.
(If the subject begins to signal double arm, have to prevent that from happening and regain control again repeated suggestion, this time with greater force.)

Case 1 B. If the challenge fist fails, to regain control.
(If the subject gives signal try to open the first have to prevent that from happening and regain control again repeated suggestion, this time with greater force.)

Case 2 A. If the challenge is achieved, continues to deepen:
(The subject cannot bend the arm, then we succeeded, now we continue deepening the next level)

> *You try to bend your arm, but you cannot. That's right, you're doing fine. The more you try, the harder and harder it will fold and more and more solid, rigid and motionless becomes your arm; that's what you've accomplished.*

Case 2. If not, finding failure:
(The student cannot open his fist, then we succeeded, now we continue deepening the next level)

> *You try to open the fist, but cannot. That's right, you're doing fine. The more you try, the harder and harder it will open and more and more glued, fused and tight turns your fist; that's what you've accomplished.*

Case 1 Negotiate out of the conflict (In case you cannot bend your arm) launched a new challenge to deepen the hypnotic state

When I count to three doubles over your arm again, but I still sleep deeper and deeper. 1, 2, 3, bend your arm, and sleep!

Case 2 Negotiating out of the conflict (In case you cannot open the fist) to launch a new challenge to deepen the hypnotic state

When I count to three open your fist again, but I still sleep deeper and deeper. 1, 2, 3, Open your fist, and sleep!

Ready apprentice, and you got the idea, right? Remember that this challenge is a "proof of suggestibility" Now start your challenge of this family Psicoconflictiva. Are you ready, if true. Then we continue.

It is now where it enters your apprentice imagination; when creating, designing and innovating new techniques of this Psicoconflictiva Family. You can replace the closed fist:

- *Prohibition of opening the mouth or speak.*
- *Prohibition to get up or move from one place.*
- *Prohibition of opening the eyes, eye catalepsy, etc.*

These techniques are called catalepsy or "Catalepsy Members", that is part of your body it becomes rigid, solid and immovable, to orders, suggestions and inductions the hypnotist. a Circle of power, or Strength Level Authority Level "FP4" and "FP5" and above in the Z2 state, MEDIUM or cataleptic hypnotic trance is required (State ZETA / THETA = 4 to 7 Hz)

Observe the rotation of the characteristic language of the challenge in this test: **The keywords are: << ATTEMPT TO … YOU CAN NO LONGER … >>**

Operation and detection States

How does this fourth family work? Families Psicoconflictiva This is one of the techniques used as "proof of Suggestibility". (That is, they are not a downrigger state, but a "Suggestibility tests" to assess the degree of hyper-suggestibility subject.

So, we could use them at the beginning of our hypnosis sessions therapeutic clinical or presentation show of street hypnosis or show, so as to prepare the minds of people to take orders, inductions and suggestions of a circle power level Force or Authority level higher level (FP1, FP2, FP3) and above).

I recommend (from experience) using this Family Psicoconflictiva as "Test Suggestibility initial" After testing FALL BACK is another very effective and efficient "test Suggestibility" with a 90% chance of success that allows us to then deepen the hypnotic experience with other families from which we have already discussed above.

This family Psicoconflictiva is very useful for passing the normal state Z0 to Z1, Z2 and Z1 to. I use this trick to achieve this: Once the two (2) or three (3) "Suggestibility test" earlier, continued with the deepening of the state with another family to pass the subject to the state Z1 or Z2. Specifically, I use the technique FAMILY PSICOIMAGINARIA either of the "ship sailing the ocean, the elevator floor to floor or level slips level down, or the escalator that goes down step by step and down to reaching levels below. Whoever you choose will be fine, just remember to dominate your competition and your verbal (speaking ability).

IMPORTANT (Remember the state level Z1 is not worth us as downrigger states, since it is only preparatory hypnotic initial state to start receiving suggestions and inductions of a circle power level Force or Authority Level Higher Level (FP1, FP2, FP3) and above). To me, I like to use these "Suggestibility tests" to assess the degree of commitment of the person, detecting the level hyper-suggestibility of the subject. Since they applied correctly are perfect to help assimilate knowledge, improve concentration, relaxation, etc. Whenever suggestions are positive, affirmative, progressive, which are those that belong to the state Z1, as suggestions (inhibition) or prohibitions belonging to the state Z2 with a circle power

When we use the Psicoconflictiva Family; We launched a challenge, which is the "Testing Suggestibility" If not, you must be sure that we are in Z1. But if it works, and do it (do not get, bend the arm or open fist. And the count of three, will you order you bend your arm or open the fist and sleep. And the subject [sleep That is, enters a state of deep hypnotic trance]) So that means we have achieved the subject accept a (inhibition) ban, and as the state bans are accepted is the Z2, we know that the subject passage of state Z1 to the next level; that is, I go and is now in the Z2 state "ready to receive state downriggers and suggestions (inductions) of a circle power Strength Level or Level Authority level.

EXPLANATION: You have to make the subject through the "Testing Suggestibility" between the Z1 state, as we see it obeys positive, affirmative and progressive suggestions, and we managed to convince that his arm is so light that begins to rise upwards. Having done that, we know for sure that is in Z1. Now you practice and test the "Test Suggestibility" the Psicoconflictiva Family.

Once achieved this challenge, you know you have said that the subject has entered the Z2 state. (See, use the Psicoconflictiva family as "Suggestibility test" to see if we have reached the Z2 state). Remember that when using the technique of Psicoconflictiva Family, can number the technique. You can make the fist, to which has the arm extended and so rigid that it cannot bend, or vary and make the heavy hand, so heavy that it cannot lift it, or induction of double directional hands, etc.

> *A trick*: *Try to see the induction as a state in which the unconscious of the subject begins to believe the suggestions given by the hypnotist. Once you accept our orders, suggestions and inductions, we know for sure that is in the state Z1 ready to be brought in now to Z2.*

As I mentioned earlier, there are other families, but these four (4) I have taught you, are the most interesting and effective. Above all, they are the ones I use most. For example, test fall backward, can be used as induction technique and be found in the fifth POLYVALENT Family.

EXERCISES:

Create, write and design the wording of hypnosis technique that belongs to the family Psicoconflictiva we have studied in this lesson. Ie, innovate your own "test Suggestibility". (Check on our levels of creativity, intuition, imagination and responsiveness ...)

(XD Apprentice, no solution either for this exercise.); *so again, it's your time to take action and make things happen. Remember the power is within you, and you have the information you already have the steps just need you to take it into practice and demonstrate your wit, creativity, intuition and desire to become one of the best hypnotists.*

So, go ahead apprentice, I know you can, I believe in you, in your potential and your ability to perform these exercises I propose. APPRENTICE So, go ahead and let's get down to work and perform this exercise.

XD apprentice keep in mind that everything's up to you! So far, they have done extremely well. And I know you will continue to improve, you and I together, we will achieve great things with this course. I'm giving my best for you, now you put the best they can give and I know you will go far.

Good **LEARNERS**, we have **reached the end of this fourth chapter!** I hope you liked and above all you have learned a lot with this fourth (4) techniques *"Big Eight Families of Hypnosis" study techniques adapted from the book "{[Eric Barone and Jacques Mandorla in his ABC of Hypnosis (Develop Your Mental Potential) of Editions Tikal]}". As* always apprentice, I wish you luck with the previous year. The domain of each of the four (4) "Techniques" of the Families of hypnosis, is what will allow you to take your hypnotic abilities to the next level. Remember, if you have any questions for exercise, *(You know you can always count on me, for what you need)* Remember that "*If you have any questions, you can "email me directly to my mail (E-mail)*".

MásterCoach.YlichTarazona@gmail.com
http://www.reingenieriamentalconpnl.com

Well, I hope to read your messages from the "Comments" section of my website Oh! APPRENTICE, I would also like you to comment me the experience you had when testing suggestibility "Stiff Arm or Closed Fist "from "Proof of Suggestibility" the Psicoconflictiva Family. Until next apprentice- I hope to have news soon yours ... ^ _ ^!

If you enjoyed this workshop hypnosis, and want to "help" with your contribution, to support me to continue doing this wonderful work, which, with love, prepared for you. You can do this through the following link.

http://bit.ly/PaypalDonación
Thank you for your contribution

SUCCESS IS FOR THOSE THAT WE ARE WILLING TO PAY THE PRICE AND ENJOY THE ROAD
"Success is more than one condition is a state of mind. Success is a journey; It is the consecutive achievement of small goals, and is the result of a life with purpose. And so, our goals are carried out; We must be willing to set our minds toward our destination, take action, implement the plan or project life and make things happen.
-. YLICH TARAZONA. -

SIMPLIFIED TECHNICAL FAMILY TO MAKE FAST HYPNOSIS

Are there some quick and effective techniques to hypnotize in less than a minute?

Of course,". So, you wonder apprentice ...¿*Why not, we've talked before them? Why use more of our time, doing all the techniques families you have shown us, if they require much greater amount of time? Why let these advanced techniques, to teach them in the end? Good questions, the answer is simple. Why are you* **SIMPLIFIED HYPNOSIS TECHNIQUES TO MAKE FAST HYPNOSIS**, deserve to have more experience, knowledge, practice and mastery of the previous families. *But mostly apprentice, because these* **simplified hypnosis techniques for rapid hypnosis** *They have a degree higher than their predecessor's difficulty and need to have a greater degree of charisma, confidence, security and expertise in the proper use of levels and degrees of hypnosis ... and the ability to effectively master the art of ALLURE and suggestion.*

Let's briefly review:

Recall that the "state Z1" *Only accepts positive, affirmative and progressive suggestions and is divided into two levels deep are:*

STATE HIPNOIDAL *or Z0 and Z1 incantation,* *Brainwave* **ALPHA / ALPHA = 8 to 13 Hz** *or* **(Cycles per second or cps)**
LIGHTWEIGHT trancelike state conducive to start performing self-hypnosis, hypnosis practice and is a favorable state to receive and accept simple suggestions, positive affirmations, progressive inductions and hypnotic patterns basic circle power or force level Authority Level "FP1" and "FP2".

hypnotic state that occurs naturally or created, for example:
- ✓ Seeing a movie, going to the movies, listen to certain music.
- ✓ While we recite a prayer or a mantra.
- ✓ While we dive into reading a good book.
- ✓ When we are in love - infatuation or enchantment.

It is characterized by the following HYPNOTICS PHENOMENA
- ✓ Mental relaxation
- ✓ Physical relaxation
- ✓ Partial decreased breathing
- ✓ Partial decreased pulse or heartbeat
- ✓ Feeling mild lethargy
- ✓ Feeling faint catalepsy

And the state **Superficial mild hypnotic trance Z1**, *Brainwave* ZETA / THETA = 4 to 7 *Hz or* **(Cycles per second or cps)**

State conducive to accept and receive a larger amount and direct and mild suggestive inductions and hypnotic patterns and commands a circle progressive power level Authority Level Strength or suggestions "FP3" and "FP4".

It is characterized by the following HYPNOTICS PHENOMENA
- ✓ Greater control of emotions and feelings
- ✓ Decreased breathing, this slows
- ✓ gradual decrease of the pulse or heart rate
- ✓ Feeling of lethargy or mental and physical sluggishness
- ✓ Ocular sensation catalepsy and tips

Close your eyes and increase the number of blink

****

What kind of suggestions they are accepted in the "State Z2" *Allowed to accept inhibitions and (Suggestions Ban) and is divided into two levels deep they are:*

HYPNOTIC TRANCE MEDIUM or cataleptic Z1 and Z2, *Brainwave* ZETA / THETA = 4 to 7 Hz or (cycles per second)

It is suitable to receive and accept a greater number of suggestions, inductions and direct through hypnotic patterns circle power level Force or Authority Level "FP5" and "FP6" subjective orders.

It is characterized by the following HYPNOTICS PHENOMENA
- ✓ Hypnotic phenomenon Anesthesia and Analgesia Low and Medium (tolerance and capacity susceptible to relieve and control certain degree of pain) Effect Fakir - carried over needle, local surgical anesthesia.
- ✓ Amnesia light and medium, ability to forget certain ideas or simple, such as names, dates, numbers, colors, smells, tastes and events.
- ✓ Ability to maintain Hypnotic Trance Medium or cataleptic, either with eyes open or closed.
- ✓ This status Hypnotic or cataleptic Middle It allows the subject to accept an inhibition (A slight ban) start leaving such a bad habit.
- ✓ ONIRICAL state or state *TWILIGHT* conducive to stimulate, create maintain lucid dreams, astral travel and extra cause bodily experiences.

****

And the state of TRANCE HYPNOTIC THRESHOLD somnambulic or somnambulism Z2 = DELTA brainwaves Between 0.5 to 3 *Hz or* **(Cycles per second or cps),**

It is suitable to receive and accept a greater number of suggestions, inductions and subjective through hypnotic patterns and commands a circle power level Force or Authority Level "FP7" and "FP8" direct orders.

It is characterized by the following HYPNOTICS PHENOMENA
- ✓ *State conducive to creating hypnotic phenomena and stimulate "Hyper - suggestibility"" Hyper-creativity "and" hyper-concentration "* **allowing the emergence of ideo motor responses, sensory ideo, and ideo-emotional** *amplifying the response levels and deepening the evocative experiences and sensory, physical and mental extra.*
- ✓ Ability to develop Phenomenon Hypnotic Analgesia and Anesthesia moderate, overall pain control, ability to walk on burning coals, traversed with pins and tolerance have contact with fire and ice.

✓ Hypnotic phenomenon Lethargy, Catalepsy and Catatonic moderate and high cataleptic limbs or entire body.

✓ **State of hyper - suggestibility** "It is a superior amplification response or downrigger the suggestive experiences or state of hyper concentration and total relaxation that is metaphorically associated with deep slumber, the latter called hypnotic trance state.

****

FASCINATION as a tool used in hypnosis, is the resource that allows us to try to divert the critical factor of consciousness of the subject in order to implement the suggestion (covert orders) directly into the subconscious mind of the person through various techniques of Visual Perception, auditory, or kinesthetic sensory so that suggestions (covert orders) are more easily processed by the subject's unconscious.

SUGGESTION is "{(Order Covert)}" that by the LANGUAGE both verbal and nonverbal (posture "look, gestures", "Symmetry" - "Orientation" - "Tilt" - "cocked" and "Micro-Facial Expressions ") allow us to generate subliminal and subjective orders entitling us access to the subconscious mind and the unconscious of the person. In other words, suggestion, are "covert orders" generated through verbal and nonverbal language in a subtle way, that distracts the critical factor of the mind and allows us to embed commands to the subconscious so that it accepts them more easily.

Ready apprentice; after this brief summary, we are ready to begin mastering and know the variants **Fast and effective techniques to hypnotize in less than one minute**. We can find these methodologies in advanced hypnosis *family Psicoconflictiva*.

Fast techniques of Psicoconflictiva Family and Derivatives:

The **Fast and effective techniques to hypnotize in less than one-minute** Family Psicoconflictiva are less risky, but they tend to be the most difficult to perform by the hypnotist. *To develop these techniques Fast, you must have absolute control of the levels and degrees of Hypnosis and Fascination domain and suggestion.*

Such technical Fast, the Psicoconflictiva Family are based on PRE-SUGGESTION. But what is this?

As we have seen in previous chapters partially; and study deeper in later chapters, the PRE-SUGGESTION are all suggestions *(Covert orders) that the subject himself is given to hypnotize.*

<u>Let me share AN EXAMPLE</u>: *Imagine the following scenario. Imagine an adult, serious, respectable person, known in the media as an important person, always dressed elegantly, and claims to be one of the best hypnotists in the world. And one day; very emphatic way you approach someone who knows or has heard of him and his fame as a hypnotist, and this is about confidence, looks into her eyes for a minute and nothing snaps fingers and you say you sleep. (At that time subject to hypnotize, has received many pre-suggestions. Go to the hypnotist knows hypnotize, has heard of his fame as a hypnotist, observes his appearance and serious appearance, confident, safe and smart. He knows in his unconscious; that when the hypnotist makes some sign and say some magic words like SLEEPS, which you will be ordering the person is to fall asleep). Given; These pre-suggestions in mind, the end result will be hypnotized person.*

The majority of **<u>Fast and effective techniques to hypnotize in less than one minute</u>**, Work that same way ... *That is to say; once we create our reputation as a hypnotist, we become more effective in our presentations, as people unconsciously predisposing and pre-beguile to follow the instructions of least resistance, and with a greater degree of suggestibility allowing us to be more effective when generating and create instant hypnotic phenomena. Now you may ask ... Well and where we are starting our way as a hypnotist, as we can also leverage the power of the PRE-SUGGESTIONS? ...*

The answer is simple apprentice, believe that credibility from the moment you begin your clinical hypnosis sessions or hypnosis shows your show ... ***And how do I do you ask?*** Good simple apprentice; using your charisma, wit, security and confidence when you present yourself, when you make small talk or interview "pre-hypnotic", when the doubts, myths, fears and concerns about hypnosis, showing your knowledge, your mastery of the subject. *That slowly, you'll be allowing to generate in the subconscious mind of the person the image you want to project. And if you endorse that image with your body language, verbal and nonverbal; and you keep at all times your charisma, wit, confidence and trust in line with what you say and projecting through your actions ... Then apprentice, you've begun to hypnotize the unconscious minds of people, resulting in that when starting to make* **convincing**, Testing Suggestibility, undercover tests and Downriggers Hypnotic States people will pay more attention, removed their psychological barriers and you will provide them greater opportunities to believe in yourself and follow your guide, instructions, suggestions, orders and inductions, positioning yourself and finally consolidating as the hypnotist before your eyes ... *And that apprentice, and is a great achievement in your practice of* **<u>*Fast and effective techniques to hypnotize in less than one minute*</u>**. *Why? Because to position yourself as an expert in the eyes of the people, they themselves began to pre-suggestible ... Do you understand the power of what I'm teaching?*

Now if an apprentice, let's start with our <u>TECHNICAL QUICK and effective to mesmerize in less than one minute</u>. Such techniques Psicoconflictiva family are mainly based on suggestion and pre-suggestion.

<u>Test lock eyeballs, eyelids heavy or Catalepsy Eye:</u>

This technique Quick suggestion, known as catalepsy eye, is a "test Suggestibility" having a strong psychological stimulation component (Hiper-Suggestibility and inductive response) ...

> **Yes, in September**: *A technique used to get put the subject on our side, and who agrees with us at least 3 "YES" followed ("covert orders").*
>
> ***FOR EXAMPLE****: You can sit / stand "Yes", you can raise your legs / feet "Yes", you can take a deep breath "Yes". From that moment, it will be much simpler than your subconscious mind accesses our suggestions of rapid techniques more freely hypnosis, preparing to begin the hypnotic process.*
>
> *Always remember to project your image in harmony with your body, verbal and non-verbal language; and maintain at all times your charisma, wit, creativity, intuition, security and confidence consistent with what you say, think and do ...*

The steps then apply Yes in September are as follows:

<u>Step 2</u>: *I want you to relax, take a deep breath, inhales and exhales, Inhale - Exhale, Inhale - Exhale. So is; right, you're doing fine. Now I want you to take another deep breath; but this time, releasing the air, I want you to look a bit down, in a position of your head that you are and you feel comfortable and let your eyes close completely, press them tightly, also close your eyelids tightly, you have pressure your eyes and eyelids to stick together completely, again lobbying to join and fully merge, and let your eyelids and your eyes close completely, totally. Perfect; That's right, you're doing very well.*

<u>Step 1</u>: The hypnotist secure and confident manner is placed in front of the subject *(Patient or participant); and he says with a firm voice, he looked into her eyes. (While the hypnotist must at all times keep your eyes without blinking and staring at the point just between the eyebrows of the subject (third eye), but located far behind his head. Evidencing the hypnotist, it can and is through his view the subject's head to hypnotize)*

It should thus be maintained for a few seconds. Then, while still looking into his eyes staring, surely gives the following suggestion:

Step 2: Relax and breathe deeply, *"Now you feel like you weigh much your eyelids ... You cannot keep your eyes open for longer ... immediately start to close ... You start to get very tired ... You're very sleepy ... now you go into a trance very deep hypnosis sleep! "*

Just short, right?

RECOMMENDATIONS: I advise you to avoid attempting this method of rapid hypnosis, until you've mastered to perfection all the other techniques.

Hitherto this lesson fast and effective techniques to hypnotize in less than a minute! Apprentice, I hope that everything I've written so far, has been of interest to you ... Remember to take action, if you want things to happen ... Be full of courage, arm yourself with courage, believe in yourself, follow my recommendations, and see as you can hypnotize anyone, anytime and anywhere with this technique.

Ahh! I forgot! An apprentice of this course practice hypnosis, has asked me to put on the website about audio files to MP3 with my voice, who personally show the different tones of voice that I use in my hypnosis sessions and in my shows show. I think it's a very good idea! And I am already preparing audio for upload ... Also, I'll upload some videos live personally practicing the various techniques of hypnosis I've been teaching them ... I hope you like and enjoy, but mostly you get the most out ... "In the end, I preparing a HYPNOSIS COURSE COMPLETELY audio and video "so you should be aware ...

It has also occurred to me, a wonderful idea; such apprentice if you can record the techniques I've taught in different families with different tones and volumes of voice, and then I send it to my personal email MásterCoach.YlichTarazona@Gmail.Com Then I will select each of which you may command me, the better tone in the different techniques and families of hypnosis and I will publish on the website along with the name of its author. And the first 10 people to send them to me, together with a home video performing one of the techniques will be participating in a lottery, who engages live on the platform of Google Hangouts, so that the winning participants a full course PROFESSIONAL hypnosis takes AUDIO, VIDEO AND PDF, completely free gift, the value of the actual course is valued at more than $ 350 ...

Another thing! Apprentice, if you think what I'm doing is worth it, you are learning a lot, and I have given all the best to teach them how it should be; and want to support me, to bring these teachings to more people like you want to learn to become an excellent hypnotist. Then send me an email to the email address above. And I will answer personally to your mail telling you anything you can do to pushing me and helping me to continue taking this course of hypnosis practice around the world, it would be great right? And most importantly (It will not cost money. Only about five to 10 minutes of your time) and you've already made your

bit in this great mission that together you and I are going to bring more people ... Since this work, I have been doing that really takes me quite some time,
^ _ ^ / =)

The time it takes to post the next chapter, will depend on how is your collaboration in this great project. For now, Apprentice, later!

Good **LEARNERS**, we have **reached the end of this special lesson**! I hope you liked and above all they have learned a lot with these powerful **TECHNICAL QUICK and effective to mesmerize in less than one minute**. As always apprentice, I wish you luck in your practice. Mastering this ***SIMPLIFIED TECHNIQUE TO MAKE FAST HYPNOSIS*** *It is what will allow you to take your hypnotic skills to the next level.* Remember, if you have any questions for exercise, *(You know you can always count on me, for what you need)* Remember that "*If you have any questions, you can "email me directly to my mail (E-mail)*".

MásterCoach.YlichTarazona@gmail.com
http://www.reingenieriamentalconpnl.com

Well, I look forward to reading your message in the "Comments" section of my website Oh! APPRENTICE, I would also, as always currents experience I lived when performing **TECHNICAL QUICK and effective to mesmerize in less than one-minute** Lock the eyepieces, heavy-lidded eyes or Catalepsy Globes. Until next apprentice chapter- I hope to have news soon yours ... ^ _ ^!

If you enjoyed this workshop hypnosis, and want to "help" with your contribution, to support me to continue doing this wonderful work, which, with love, prepared for you. You can do this through the following link.

http://bit.ly/PaypalDonación
Thank you for your contribution

"I never said it easy, but I promise you it will not be impossible ... You just have to be willing to pay the price of success and then enjoy the results the rest of his entire life." - YLICH TARAZONA. -

CHAPTER FIVE: WORK PROGRAM TO BECOME AN EXCELLENT MESMER:

Hello such apprentice, and we have reached the fifth chapter of our course of practice hypnosis, first, I will congratulate you for having come to this lesson. This means that you actually are interested in learning hypnosis and become one of the best hypnotists. And I have good news, you're on the right track. So, without further ado let's continue our next lesson on your way to excellence in this wonderful art of hypnosis.

Rules 15 Hypnotic Suggestion:

1. **BRIEF**. Our brain can process data simultaneously five, and even seven, but not ten, or twenty. For this reason, the must avoids building suggestions and long inductions such as: "The heaviness of your arm moves first toward his left foot, then to his right hand, before reaching his forehead, finally returning to his left foot". It is better to say: "The heaviness of her arm, a little bit shifted towards its foot." "The heaviness of her foot, moves very slowly toward his hand," etc. Do you see are the same suggestions and inductions, but declared shorter and accurately?

2. **PARTICULAR and ACCURATE**. He will say: "His arm is getting heavier and heavier as lead," "Your hand every time becomes more and more rigid as a steel rod," "Your eyes are becoming heavier and heavier, her eyelids they close and feel the sensation of entering into a deep sleep. "

3. **AFFIRMATIVE IN THIS TIME**. As if what we said was happening at this time in the here and NOW: "It feels heavy or tired; you feel relaxed or calm. " Better not say, "I would like you to feel heaviness in ..."

4. **POSITIVE**. The suggestion will be accepted much better, the greater the improvement that provides the individual: an example of how it should not be: "We will prevent any disease by quitting smoking." Instead, an example of how SI should be: "Your lungs are cleared, your breathing is energetic, his urge to smoke decrease and you feel more and healthier".

5. **REPEATED**. If a subject is told that his body is heavy directly (your body is heavy, your body is heavy, too heavy ...) it is more likely that we will finally provoke lust. The right thing would be to say as follows: "His body gradually becomes more and more light, your body now begins to feel completely light, becoming lighter and lighter, his legs and hands also It is becoming more and lighter gradually. Each of my words, makes both your body, legs and arms, and feel even lighter. So, light you feel the sensation of levitating, so light that it feels completely relaxed "(As you see we are saying the same thing but differently)

<u>**6.**</u> **SIMPLE or SUPERIMPOSED**. These two tools, is to relate a fact to another (though in fact have no relationship to each other)

SIMPLE "His arm is becoming lighter and lighter."

SUPERIMPOSED "The lighter your arm becomes, the deeper he sinks into sleep; lighter between his arm becomes more and more relaxes your body and more and more feel a sense of deep sleep. "

This superimposed suggestion, as you may notice makes the relationship a simple suggestion. As you saw in the inductions, there is actually a real relationship between the two; It is the ability of the hypnotist conviction that creates it.

<u>**7.** **Immediate or delayed**</u>:

DEFERRED "After counting up to three you lift up your left arm."

IMMEDIATE "Raise your left arm now."

Deferred has two advantages: 1 allows preventing the subject, especially regarding physical contact if necessary; and thus, avoid generating some excitement. 2nd But in itself, used properly, is another hypnotic action that drives the individual to respond before an order and provide another reality ... Through the simple power of their imagination and hyper-suggestibility.

Also, it has two immediate advantages: 1 View the degree of attention and suggestibility of the subject before direct orders. 2nd to assess the level of hypnosis where the subject is. If you respond immediately to the order of "Raise your left arm" means is in the state Z2.

<u>**8.** **INTRAHIPNÓTICA or posthypnotic**</u>:

INTRAHIPNÓTICA: It occurs during hypnosis. (Ie, are hypnotic phenomena that occur during hypnosis).

posthypnotic: Refers to the time after hypnosis. (That is, are the orders and hypnotic suggestions, which are maintained even after finishing the hypnosis session). For example:

> *"From now on, whenever you touch the forehead and tell you to sleep, you will enter a state of deep hypnotic trance even more, than you are now. Now, to prove that you understood, accepted and assimilated everything I've told you, I'm going to count to three (3) and wake up. And you will see that you will find you well and you will feel full of energy and vitality; but even after waking up, whenever you touch the forehead and tell you to sleep, you close your eyes and again enter a state of hypnosis further and deeper than you are now, if you understand nods.*

ONCE CREATED THE ORDER; and the subject wakes up, test the suggestion posthypnotic, will pass the slight hand and gently across the face (activating the kinesthetic anchor) and tell SLEEPS (activating auditory and sensory anchor) and if the person understood, accept and assimilate all order was implemented was previously re-enter the state of deep hypnotic trance agreed. And ready, we will have already achieved the goal. That's good, right?

9. **PROGRESSIVE**. If you tell someone once: "Your relaxed body", you may need to repeat it for fifteen minutes to that feeling really believe in the subconscious of the person. But if you start saying, "Your body starts to relax slowly, feeling like your hands relax more and more, your legs feel like relaxing more and more." "Right, so you're doing very well." "Now you feel peace and tranquility in all your being, feel a sense of well-being throughout your body, now feels that peace, tranquility and feeling of well-being is felt throughout the body and mind, etc." Apprentice, as you can see now we can get the same result as above, but this time, we should only use a maximum of about five minutes and ready.

10. **REASONABLE**. You always have to anticipate and avoid stressful situations. FOR EXAMPLE: Never shall say, "You are immersed in a deep sleep that covers gradually" to a subject that has been saved from drowning in the sea a few years earlier, as this type of suggestion could cause anxiety. The right thing would be to use INDETERMINATE phrases or unspecific, ie using neutral phrases like: "You slowly relax, feel at peace, calm, your body and your mind begins to feel feelings of well-being, that is, so it is, feels like the feeling of tranquility travels throughout your body, now you feel like you relax more and deeper, feels like the feeling of relaxation allows you to enter gradually into a state of deep sleep, so, right you are doing it very well.

11. **FLEXIBLE**. In order to adapt to every situation, context or circumstance, as the occasion demands. We must be flexible to adapt our vocabulary and diction at the same dialect word or subject to hypnotize.

12. **CONVERGING interrelated**. Our suggestions should be consistent with each other, and have a continuous pattern related to the above, to bring the subject finally to the desired hypnotic state. For example: "Your body relaxes, her eyelids weighed and his eyes closed, little heart gradually reduced their rhythm, their breathing slows more and more" is said to converge as each of the suggestions mentioned above stimulate in the subject unconscious memory of the feeling of sleep, leading him to feel the sensation of sleep. As every action mentioned above (representing five natural physiological consequences of sleep) so successfully used this technique, we can artificially create the sensation that occurs in the physiological sleep, using that feeling in our favor.

13. **REALIZABLE**. If we gave a suggestion that may not be realizable by the subject. Such that (go against their principles, morality, ethics, religion or morals …) In these cases, can happen: 1 Nothing; 2nd The subject wakes up; or 3 ° The subject runs away and takes refuge in the state Z3. For this reason, it is always advisable to give orders, suggestions and inductions that are within their (principles, morality, ethics, religion and morals …) and especially in the correct state Z1 and Z2 and circle of power, strength level or correct level of authority.

14. **Reasonable, consistent and coherent**. Always it has to anticipate physiological reactions. FOR EXAMPLE: We cannot tell the subject that your fingers will begin to separate, when hands are completely open.

15. **NORMAL or SUBLIMINAL**. A Normal suggestion is meant to be consciously heard by the subject. Lie is a subtle subliminal suggestion and subjectively directed to the subconscious of the person. Normal Suggestions are for example: simple and direct orders, you feel relaxed, your arm levitates, your hands get stuck, your eyes close, your eyelids weigh, etc. While subliminal suggestions are, for example: Invisible images interleaved in a movie, sentences pronounced at high speed or in a tone so low that they cannot hear, or a subtle suggestion or covert order as could be "Every time you hear my voice, you will feel more and more relaxed.

As we could assimilate in this section apprentice, LAS 15 HYPNOTIC SUGGESTION RULES are vital. Learning these 15 principles and adapt them to our sessions of clinical hypnosis therapist or at our shows of street hypnosis show will allow us to be more likely to succeed in our hypnotic's processes.

Now to continue, they teach you the right steps in a hypnosis session, so they can adapt to their own therapies. Apprentice, so without further ado let's start with our next lesson.

Part Two: HYPNOSIS SESSION according Viewpoint Mesmer

Now to continue, I will describe a hypnosis session from the point of view of the specialist (hypnotist) hypnotist or hypnotherapist:

We can divide it into 5 stages:

1. **Induce**;
2. **Deepen**;
3. **Hypnotic Trance phenomena or**;
4. **Suggestion** Posthypnotic or intervention;
5. **Procedure Awakening**;

<u>1.</u> *Induce: It means placing the subject in the state Z1.*

<u>2.</u> *Deepen: Corresponds to make you pass the state Z2.*

<u>3.</u> *Hypnotic Trance phenomena or: This is the level where the set target is reached (heal an ailment, learn or teach a skill, overcome a habit or develop a more empowered, to create anesthesia, analgesia, catalepsy, etc.) thanks to have succeeded in increasing the* **CIRCLE OF POWER** *or Level Strength (FP3 and FP4) to a higher level of authority or higher FP5 and Higher*

<u>4.</u> *Posthypnotic suggestion of Intervention: The essential element of hypnosis. It is when the subject (viewer) patient or participant It is in the transition between states Z1 to Z2, and we can give posthypnotic orders that extend and run once you've awakened. And orders remain in force once the session is complete, even on days or later dates.*

This is very interesting, I'll share an example: "From now on, whenever you touch the forehead (creating a kinesthetic anchor - touch with your hands) and tell you to sleep (create an auditory anchor - with the word SLEEPS) you enter a state of deep hypnotic trance even more, which you are now (create a sensory anchor - feel completely relaxed). Now, to prove that you understood, accepted and assimilated everything I've told you, I'm going to count to three (3) and wake up. And you will see that you will find you well and you will feel full of energy and vitality; but whenever you touch the forehead and tell you to sleep, close your eyes and go into a state of hypnosis further and deeper. Story: 1're regaining your energy and vitality; 2 you are very good and you feel sensational, and you're waking up more and more; 3 you can wake up active and ready to continue, awake now. "...

ONCE CREATED THE ORDER; and the subject (viewer) patient or participant wakes up, test the suggestion posthypnotic will pass the slight hand and gently across the face (activating the kinesthetic anchor) and tell SLEEPS (activating auditory and sensory anchor) and if the person understood, accept and assimilate the entire order was to be implemented before, re-enter the state of deep hypnotic trance agreed. AND READY have achieved the goal you understand the idea? Do you understand the potential of posthypnotic suggestion? ...

<u>5.</u> *Procedure Awakening*. The process of awakening, is the most important at the end of our hypnotic session, as it is the action that allows us to cancel all that has been practiced or enacted in the hypnosis session. But keeping only the posthypnotic suggestion if any. For this reason, because of its importance, this must be done or done slowly, and never awaken the subject(Viewer) patient or participant and a fast or abruptly. Most ideally, as follows: "When I count to three

(3) awaken the state in which you are now, and you wake up alert, ready, attentive and energy and welfare 100% of your optimum performance, you're READY "Story: 1're regaining your energy and vitality! 2 you are very good and you feel sensational, and you're waking up and activating your 5 senses growing; 3 you can wake up and active and ready to continue, awake now. "...

NOTE: *As we begin the process of awakening, it is advisable while we counting (1, 2, 3 ...) gradually increase the tone and volume of our voice and engage our pace and rhythm of what we are saying in consistency feeling, emotion and experience that we are inducing the person. Thus, the subject (viewer) patient or participant in our words, actions and expressions experiences we want to convey.*

SYNTHESIS "Before, During and After a hypnosis session"

1. **BEFORE THE HYPNOSIS** Make a previous interview, have a pre-hypnotic talk, write the medical report, read and complete the therapeutic script with the patient or participant, fill the contract or posthypnotic agreement to keep in mind the goals they want to achieve with the session, deepen the reason for the consultation or session, ask questions on the subject to locate possible psychological and physiological if any problems, detect fears, traumas, phobias, expectations, desires and interests, etc. Do you understand what I'm saying? By doing all this, you can not only prevent any problems with time, but above all you can come on and cover any expectation, positioning yourself as an expert in the field and strengthen your image as Hypnotist, Hypnotist, hypnotist or hypnotherapist. It is clear, that having a profile of the staff concerned who are going to work, you'll have more advantages, if not you would fulfill with all these initial procedures do I give me to understand? You agree that, by having more information, more likely to have success in carrying out your therapeutic clinical hypnosis sessions and more likely to have success to make your shows of street hypnosis or show. Are you clear on this truth? Knowing this, you'll avoid someone who has a phobia to water the method of the boat. XD - very careful with that. more likely to have success in carrying out your therapeutic clinical hypnosis sessions and more likely to have success to make your shows of street hypnosis or show. Are you clear on this truth? Knowing this, you'll avoid someone who has a phobia to water the method of the boat. XD - very careful with that. more likely to have success in carrying out your therapeutic clinical hypnosis sessions and more likely to have success to make your shows of street hypnosis or show. Are you clear on this truth? Knowing this, you'll avoid someone who has a phobia to water the method of the boat. XD - very careful with that.

2. **During hypnosis**: Induce, deepen, creating hypnotic phenomena, perform post-hypnotic suggestion, successfully complete the procedures of awakening, Increase Circle of Power or Strength Level one (FP1, FP2 and FP3) to a higher level of authority or higher FP5 and higher , testing suggestibility, covert tests, inductions, convincing and downriggers of hypnotic states, choose the state of

hypnotic trance we want to achieve according to our goals (STATE HIPNOIDAL or Incantation Z0 and Z1, TRANCE HYPNOTIC MILD or Superficial Z1, TRANCE HYPNOTIC MEDIUM or cataleptic Z1 and Z2 or Z2 somnambulistic THRESHOLD HYPNOTIC TRANCE as appropriate.

3.   **After hypnosis**: Have a short conversation with the subject (viewer) patient or participant, which prompted the person that has chronologically everything you remember that happened, as this allows us to detect the Z2 states, through amnesia retroactive and spontaneous posthypnotic. (This is called the temporary oblivion said before, that when entering Z2, forgot or technique that made him into a deep state (Z2) is deleted), ending a brief interview and check the contract or posthypnotic agreement verify that the objectives were met, schedule the next appointment, plan the next session of clinical or therapeutic hypnosis, planning the next show of street hypnosis or hypnosis show, recommend, offer and sell some of your teaching materials and support (Audios, Videos, Books,

Work Program to become an excellent HYPNOTIST

1. Preparation of the Voice.

Choose a text, preferably make it interesting and motivating for you; you can use as references suggestibility tests, or hypnotic inductions there in this course; and pronounces each phrase, 4 times in 4 different ways:
  - *Paternal authoritarian.*
  - *Maternal sweet and affectionate.*
  - *Collaborator.*
  - *Flexible.*

Here I will share some examples:

Paternal	Authority. "Obedience respect".	"Get up immediately!" And come here, please.
Maternal	Sweetness, Protection. "Obedience of love".	"I would like you to get up to catch that box: is that I feel very tired."
Collaborator	Analytical Intelligence. "Obedience by logical reasoning".	"That smoke can be harmful; You should get up and open the window. "Do not you think?
Flexible	Freedom of Choice, Suggested initiative. "Obedience through an apparent freedom of choice."	"Imagine getting up. Cause that desire internally to you; do it when you want and feel you should do it and do it. "

For this exercise, if necessary, the hypnotist can use these four voices in less than fifteen seconds. This gives an idea of the necessary adaptation.

It should be emphasized at this point, it is not enough just reading these suggestions; You must be aware of the imitation you do when you utter inductions, to seek to accurately pronounce the hypnotic command, through adequate Using a specific voice tone, speaking with a voice that reflects the emotion you want to wake up, describing mental images that create the subject a sense of deepening the state we want to induce.

2. Look in the mirror. Practice the previous exercise, talk to your four Paternal authoritarian voices - Maternal, sweet and loving - **Collaborator Y Flexible**.
For this two-step; looking in the mirror, tries to reflect the following:
THE BREATHING Change the style of ...

- **Rhythm** *"Balanced or uncontrolled " - "Slow or Suave"*
- **Shape** *"Abdominal or Pectoral"*
- **Volume** *"Sufficient or insufficient"*

EYE MOVEMENTS use your eyes in different directions ...

- *Upward, toward the left.*
- *Upwards, towards the right.*
- *Laterally toward the end tip of the left eye.*
- *Laterally to the tip end of the right side of the eye.*
- *Down towards the right.*
- *Down, toward the right*

MICRO-FACIAL EXPRESSIONS using your face about making gestures ...

- *"Gestures"* of doubt, fear, fear, anger, restlessness, tension, Relaxation, Excitement, Joy, security, happiness, peace, love and harmony.

BODY POSTURE, Head position and hand movements

- *"Movements of Affirmation" - "Movements of Denial"*
- *"Gestures and movements with the hands and fingers"*
- *"Hard" - "Laid" - "Quiet or Imperative"*

THE VOICE Use your voice in different style ...

- **Rhythm** *"Paused or fast"*
- **Doorbell** *"High or low"*
- **Tone** *"Smooth or Rough"*
- **Volume** *"High or low"*

3. Build Suggestions on the basis of a hypnotic state you want to generate.
To carry out this exercise, you can help by applying the sixteen rules of suggestion with which I began this chapter. Learn these sixteen rules. Read a text from one of the suggestions you've already created and ask yourself why certain suggestion would not serve sentences.

When talking; analyzes what happens if you say the phrases:
- *Very quickly / slowly*
- *With Tone Neutral / emphatic*
- *Very weak / strong*

4. Learn 5 Steps of a hypnosis session, studying States, Grades and levels of hypnosis, techniques, tools and Families of hypnosis. States a hypnosis session (Induce, deepen, hypnotic phenomena, post-hypnotic suggestion and process of awakening); States and levels of hypnosis (STATUS MONITOR "Z0" - Present here and now, neuronal level BETA = between 14 to 28 Hz or (cycles per second or cps) - STATE HIPNOIDAL or Charm Z0 and Z1, neuronal level ALPHA / ALPHA = 8 to 13 Hz or (cycles per second or fps) - TRANCE HYPNOTIC SLIGHT or Superficial Z1, neuronal level ZETA / THETA = 4 to 7 Hz or (cycles per second or fps) - TRANCE HYPNOTIC MEDIUM or cataleptic Z1 and Z2 , neuronal level ZETA / THETA = 4 to 7 Hz or (cycles per second) - HYPNOTIC TRANCE THRESHOLD somnambulic or somnambulism Z2, neuronal level DELTA = 0,5 3 Hz or (cycles per second or cps), outwardly perceptible) ; Magnetism technique (MOPPAO); Tools Mesmer (Fascination and suggestion); Family Hypnosis (Sensorial, physiological, Psicoimaginaria, Psicoconflictiva); Purpose, strategy and phraseology of the families of hypnosis.

5. Learn the Purpose, Strategy and phraseology of sensory FAMILIES, Physiological, Psicoconflictiva And Psicoimaginaria. Apprentice, for this exercise have to be able to adapt the 4 families of hypnosis to all cases. You know what each one, understand its stages and the corresponding order of each objective, strategy and phraseology.

6. Invent New Techniques Suggestions. In this exercise, the purpose is to design, create and innovate new suggestions and hypnotic from 4 families of hypnosis (sensory, physiological, Psicoconflictiva and Psicoimaginaria) using new already known and studied in this course of hypnosis techniques, or inductions. The important thing is to do it in writing and based on:
a) Purpose.
b) Strategy and
c) phraseology

7. Mastering various techniques of suggestion, and what guidance is appropriately chosen the most suitable rare each induction, depending on the situation, context and circumstances that arise.

Most hypnotists:

- Begin with a previous interview, a pre-hypnotic, talk write their medical report, they read and fill the therapeutic script with the patient or participant, fill the contract or posthypnotic agreement to keep in mind the goals they want to achieve with the session or show, deepening the reason for the consultation or session, ask questions on the subject to locate possible psychological and physiological problems, if any, detect fears, traumas, phobias, expectations, desires and interests, etc.

- Use the test of suggestibility fall back (Family Sensory) and reliable test methods to check the degree of suggestibility of the subject. To achieve better results, it is recommended (Go changing the tone, volume, tempo and rhythm of the voice to find

out which works best in that subject and adapt to each situation or context in particular) - "If the subject put some resistance, subtly you switched style voice, auditory perception, visual, kinesthetic and sensory be incorporated to stimulate the desired hypnotic state the person, and finally to achieve the goal; it begins with the deepening of using other technical or family.)

<u>Recommendations to consider each hypnosis session:</u>

- Maintain: All the techniques and methodologies that you have done well, and continue to apply them on subsequent opportunities that will arise. Remember that practice and constant repetition is the mother of teaching. One of the ways we have to perfect our techniques and methodologies is regular evaluation of our actions in each practice session hypnosis show or event show. Because every time we evaluate us, allows us to internalize the model we used to repeat the same results more excellent the next time you perform the same technique.

- ACTIVATE: Anything you could see miss, and you did not make at the meeting or previous event. It is important that every time you make a clinical hypnosis session or a hypnotic show, then you evaluate what you did right, and what probably could have done better. As this will allow you to internalize and deepen your subconscious mind technique you used; allowing in this way, keep adding to your repertoire that you might have omitted, but if you had done or had tried, I was helped make the technique more effectively and efficiently as possible.

- OFF: Everything you did in the exercise, practice, clinical hypnosis session hypnosis show or spectacle you should not have done. As in the previous steps, this point will help you evaluate what you did in a particular therapeutic hypnosis session or event, you should not have done, or you might have missed. The purpose of this part of the exercise is that once you've assessed fairly, and have identified those points that should not have added to your sessions or show; then let you go eliminating anything that is unnecessary or surplus in actual practice in the future application of hypnosis exercises with a person.

Apprentice: This exercise or three-step process [HOLD - ON and OFF] will serve to gradually perfecting your hypnotic and persuasive skills. At the same time that will allow you to observe how they respond different people well be these (patients or participants), to the persuasive verbal suggestions or hypnotic oral inductions transmits them and communicate them to generate the hypnotic trance state desired in each context or situation which you perform hypnosis.

Principles to consider before starting a hypnosis session clinic or HYPNOSIS SHOW SPECTACLE.

Apprentice, before starting to hypnotize a person, we must first begin performing a series of pre-hypnotic's protocols that allow us to significantly increase our cash success rate:

ESTABLISH HARMONY, RAPPORT AND Pacing: To achieve this, the first thing we do is clearly explain to our subject matter (patient or participant) who is and who is not hypnosis. As well as explain that you will feel or experience before, during and after the session or hypnosis show; and previously establish a close relationship between you beyond trust, so that the subject (patient or participant) allows us to access that part of your unconscious mind which is empowering them to be more relevant to the suggestions and inductions that we suggest. Thus, the subject (patient or participant) participates actively in the session or hypnosis show, without putting any psychological resistance to hypnotic commands or orders are suggesting them.

DISCONNECTION OR DISSOCIATION: The next step is to disconnect the subject (patient or participant) of the conscious part of your brain (namely, logic or rational part of your mind) of the unconscious part (ie, the suggestibility of your mind). To do this, we must begin our therapy sessions or events of street hypnosis (AS APPLICABLE) with small test exercises to prove their reaction, response, disposition and suggestibility orders before we teach them. Among the most common basic exercises that are recommended we could mention Fingers Magnetic Hands Magnetic Hands Directional Up - Down, Elevation or levitation Brazos, fall back, Catalepsy Eye, arms and legs among many others that can help us get this dissociation, and finally achieve our goal.

INTRODUCTION OF Inductions: Once done prior verification of suggestibility, we can move forward slowly in our process of hypnotic trance, beginning to use a wide variety of different verbal inductions, accompanied by hypnotic commands, suggestions and persuasive patterns that allow us to finally go running to the subject (patient or participant) to enter the desired hypnotic trance state and mental state of readiness PRE-and POS HYPNOTICAL we want to achieve with the person in question.

Induction Hypnotic is the verbal process by which the hypnotist establishes, promotes, directs and suggest the person through the power of the spoken word, to enter the subject (patient or participant) to the desired state of hypnotic trance. In other words, Hypnotic Induction is the most effective means by which the hypnotist says verbally and prepares the mental conditions required in the process of hypnosis trance medium occurs. That is, the (Hypnotic Phenomena). On another idea we can say that hypnotic induction can be defined as psychological processes or mental procedures HYPNOSIS necessary to bring a person to the state of hypnotic trance desired through the power of the spoken word declared by verbal suggestions and oral inductions they communicate the subject (patient or participant). The State of Trance Hypnotic is the state of increased suggestion or suggestibility, during which the powers of the mind criticism or critical of the mind are reduced, and subjects (patients or participants) are more likely and receptive to accept commands, patterns, suggestions, inductions, direct orders and suggestions declared by the hypnotist.

Then apprentice, I will explain some of the most important basics to keep in mind when you begin to induce hypnotic states. There are dozens of principles in the course of this book, but I will highlight only the most essential and necessary to multiply our success rate:

most important to keep in mind when starting to induce trance states Hypnotic basic elements.

AUTHORITY: Any kind of suggestion, subliminal command, hypnotic induction, request or pray direct and indirect; It is even much better and work more effectively while awake even when performed by a person in authority. FOR EXAMPLE: If a stranger sees you sitting on a park bench, and asks you to get up to sit him or her - Would you? Undoubtedly not true ... But now imagine the same situation, and try to imagine this time, the person who asks you to get up from the bench to sit someone in authority is recognized, famous, important and relevant to you. In this new situation, you probably true Sederies the bank - if true ... Why? Because it represents an authority figure or important to you. [For in the field of hypnosis it is exactly the same]. That is to say, we stand before people as an authority in the field of hypnosis; in other words, we introduce ourselves as expert hypnotists to our audience, viewers, customers or patients, for our suggestions or inductions have greater strength to the subject in question.

REPETITION: We must be repeated several times, repeatedly, in different ways and in different ways the mental states that we induce and generate the minds of people (patients or participants) who would perform the session or hypnotic show. FOR EXAMPLE: If we want the subject (patient or participant) into a state of deep relaxation trance, not enough that only we tell SLEEP, sleep or relax to produce the expected hypnotic phenomenon ... For this to really happen, we must continually repeatedly bombard your subconscious mind with verbal suggestions, subliminal commands, hypnotic inductions and direct and indirect orders that allow them to induce and generate the desired hypnotic state; namely, the state of deep trance. And to achieve that goal, repeatedly we used the words dream, go to sleep or relax, prayers organized in small Subliminal created for that purpose; in order, directing the subject to enter the desired hypnotic trance state. And the best way to do this would be as follows: On the count of 3, you ordain you to close your eyes and close your eyes desire you to relax deeply until you start to get that feeling Deep Sleep, I want as you hear my voice, and tell you go to sleep feel a sense of peace and tranquility that makes you get into a deeper and deeper relaxation, as you relax you deeper and deeper feel like you fall into a deep sleep that produces you every more and more desire to sleep, right, so you're doing very well. Perfect, now that you have entered a state of deep relaxation the more you hear my voice, more and more you travel deeper into that deep sleep that gives you serenity and inner peace that you produce that stimulates you to SLEEP DEEPLY more and more. Okay, so, you're doing it correctly. Now I'll start counting from 1 to 3 and as I count going deeper and deeper and deeper into this state of deep relaxation, and I want you perceive as with every breath you relax more and more. That's right, very good; 1 inhales deeply and feel like with every breath you full of tranquility and inner peace that gives you serenity, 2 with every desire exhalation let go of all stress and feel exhale the air from your lungs feel you release all the tensions of your body, 3 feels like more and go deeper and deeper into this state of deep relaxation, right, so you're doing very well. Perfect, now go to sleep soundly. Ready; here if we did induction properly, we have generated in the person desired trance state, now we just have to move on to the next part of induction.

RIGHT GUESS: Apprentice, should start applying simple suggestions and direct inductions. The successful combination of these suggestions and inductions will allow us to get, we make it much easier to bring the subject (patient or participant) to a state of Trace Hypnotic desired. If you manage to achieve this disassociation between your conscious and your unconscious mind hypnotic session or show we will have succeeded. And to achieve this goal, first, we must follow the previously mentioned steps, as this can create a sequence or continuity in the hypnotic process, and the greater number of successes have greater the chances of success that we get. Now since you're understanding the idea?

YES-SET TECHNIQUE: We must have put the subject (patient or participant) from us. And to achieve this goal we must ensure that the person matches the affirmative and agrees with us at least 3 "YES" followed. For example, you can sit "Yes", you can raise your legs "Yes", you can take a deep breath "Yes". From that moment, it will be much simpler than your subconscious mind accesses our suggestions and inductions more freely, which will carry out the hypnotic session or entertainment show to the next level, activating the desired hypnotic phenomena.

POSITIVE REINFORCEMENT **Apprentice How do you know the subject** *(Patient or participant) if you are performing at any given time, you are doing it correctly*? It is a question that often tends to go through the mind of the person, either consciously or unconsciously. For this reason, it is vital that the person receiving the suggestions and inductions, know what is happening, happening or done in the process of hypnotic trance, is precisely what has to happen. To do this, continually reinforce the actions of the subject (patient or participant) with positive words and statements such as: "That's very good," "excellent, you're doing great," "right, so you're doing very well". FOR EXAMPLE: If we see that suddenly makes a sudden movement, we will reinforce that action, as if that was normal, "That's great," he feels like that movement makes you enter more and more into a deep trance,

ASSOCIATION: We associate our suggestions and inductions to internal and external experiences of the subject (patient or participant). If for example there any noise outside that is out of our control, then we can use that sound in our favor; suggesting that if "Listen" any outside noise makes focusing more and more on their inner peace - If on the contrary the subject (patient or participant) makes any sudden or involuntary movement such as a slight flicker or arm movement - you can suggest that "feel" with every blink performing or each arm movement allows you to enter more and more into the desired state of hypnotic trance. And thus, we use internal and external situations of the individual, and positively associate the context of our hypnotic session,

Metaphor USE: Apprentice; Metaphors are figurative and allegorical language that works very well as an excellent persuasive resources in hypnotic communication, which allows us to subconsciously associate a desired state of mind or state of consciousness altered an everyday occurrence, allowing the subject (patient or participant) potentially stimulate SUBJECTIVE alternate reality thus helping to stimulate and develop responses get ideo motor, sensory ideo, and ideo-emotional at an unconscious level and cause activate your alternate reality SUBJECTIVE; and thus, it is much simpler than the subject (patient or participant) receives the [guidance, instruction, suggestions, hypnotic suggestions and direct or indirect inductions] that we are ordering. FOR EXAMPLE:

REPRESENTATION OF SENSORY SYSTEMS: We must adapt to sensory representational system or Sub modalities the subject (patient or participant), whether this is "Visual, is represented by what he sees; Aural represents what HEAR; or kinesthetic will represent their emotions, feelings and sensations you feel. " When the group is done HYPNOSIS then we must refer multisensory the three main states that are (sight, hearing, and sensation).

Some examples of the items that we can use in our hypnotic sessions or show performances are as follows.

notes *as everything that happens around you makes you more and more relaxed.*
Listen out *as everything that happens around you makes you more and more relaxed*
feels *as everything that happens around you makes you more and more relaxed.*

VERBAL REPRESENTATION or oral communication: The power

of the spoken word is our greatest ally apprentice; For this reason, our voice, rhythm, cadence, timbre, volume and intonation harmoniously should represent what our spoken word says. FOR EXAMPLE: If we induce or suggestible the subject (patient or participant) to a state of hypnotic sleep, we have to say phrases like: In more and more into a "dream, dream, dream DEEP" "That's very good "" excellent, you're doing great "NOW" fast asleep "

The first induction or suggestion we make a tone volume or low, soft, warm voice whispering; the second, which is the direct hypnotic command we provoke, we pronounced after reinforcement used for interleaving one pray other; but this time with a tone or volume of more loudly and with authority.

However, if we want to induce or suggest him the subject (patient or participant) to enter a state of deep relaxation, we would have to pronounce phrases and sentences composed as follows: From now on, I want you to feel as you relax DEEPLY and you feel more and more relaxed to the extent that you experience an inner peace and RELAX; So, right you're doing fine.

These phrases should then speak tone, rhythm, cadence and intonation of voice that subtly express the state of relaxation and inner peace that we want to lead within your conscious and subconscious mind.

hypnotic voice: Apprentice, as hypnotists PROFESSIONALS, whether we are (street hypnotist, hypnotists show of shows, clinical hypnotists or hypnotherapists specialists) always we have to make use of two (2) types of voice, our normal voice (which is what we use in our daily interactions) and our hypnotic voice (which is the persuasive voice we use in our sessions or show to induce trance). That way, whenever the subject (patient or participant) listen to our tone Hypnotic VOICE, will be much easier to recognize and subconsciously access the desired state of trance.

Increase Circle POWER AND YOU FORCE LEVEL (FP's): *Apprentice; Increase Circle of Power and your level of strength or level of authority to a higher level (FP) allows you to develop your hypnotic to the next level skills (another friend of mine level) Do you understand me? ... Can you imagine what you can achieve?*

This allows them to create direct and indirect orders, inductions and suggestions for optimal and effective way, gradually rising in grades HYPNOSIS. That is, they manage to ascend from the circle of power and force level or level of authority to a higher level FP0 and FP1, until FP5 and higher, which enables them to produce certain hypnotic phenomena that would otherwise be impossible.

Apprentice, this principle is one of the advanced elements MOST IMPORTANT TO CONSIDER WHEN TO DEEPEN AND INDUCE HYPNOTICS STATES IN GRADES HIGHER OF HYPNOSIS.

For this reason, apprentice, I wrote a whole chapter full on this point in particular. Hypnosis is all a masterful art and desire to share you the advanced techniques that are mostly reserved for other books and omitted many of the courses. So later, I will share whatever any (street hypnotist, hypnotist show of shows, clinical hypnotist or hypnotherapist specialist) shares publicly and openly ... Do you like the idea of learning these advanced techniques, right? Yes. Ok then, without further ado we continue.

Find your own style and develop it Apprentice; this element is the most important to keep in mind when you begin to induce and create hypnotic states. My personal experience in the wonderful world of hypnosis, has taught me that to be a good hypnotist or hypnotherapist must first become the hypnotist; ie, feel, think and act like the hypnotist who want to become. Or, in other words, see yourself as the hypnotist, Hypnotist, hypnotist or hypnotherapist who can become. Always keep your attitude, charisma, confidence and security in yourself outweigh any therapeutic script, pre-hypnotic chat, linguistic trick, induction technique, suggestion, hypnotic patterns or commands. Since these are only elements that you will use as a professional to strengthen your presentation;

To start creating your own style, the first thing to do is identify which of the different specialties Hypnotic going to choose to start your way. And these options can be: make yourself known as a hypnotist in events of street hypnosis, or become a hypnotist hypnosis show theater shows; or if you prefer so you can opt for university- be titled and professionally practice as a clinical hypnotist or hypnotherapist specialist. But whatever the decision you make, you should always prepare yourself, take action and make things happen, so that you can be the best in the area you choose.

Another thing you should do to Find your own style and develop it is to choose the type of hypnosis you will use to start your way as a hypnotist, hypnotist or hypnotherapist. Among the different and multiple options exist can specialize in: Hypnosis Classic, Hypnosis Freudian, Hypnosis Show, Hypnosis Clinic, Therapeutic Hypnosis, hypnosis induction Indirectly Ericksonian Hypnosis, Hypnosis Psycholinguistics, Hypnosis with NLP, Hypnosis Conversational or combination them according to your tastes, preferences, style and personality. And to also combine them according to the situation and occasion demands. Remember the HYPNOSIS offers endless options and unlimited chances, so you take advantage of them in your favor on your way to personal excellence.

These are just some of the most basic and important to be present at a session of hypnosis clinic or hypnotherapist basic principles, as well as in shows of street hypnosis or show. As I said before this book is only a small guide theoretical and practical reference, to introduce you to the wonderful world of hypnosis. It is for this reason I have seen fit to share with you only the most significant and important first steps and basics of hypnosis.

Good **LEARNERS**, This **It has been all for now**! Good luck with the exercises, there are several tasks you have to perform. If you have any questions for different exercises, tasks and assignments *(You know you can always count on me for anything, I'm your teacher, and I am here to guide you along the path to excellence in this wonderful journey to your destination ... WHAT IS "BECOME ONE OF THE BEST hypnotists WORLD") ...*

If there is something that may not yet understand; quiet apprentice is normal, everything is learned step by step, gradually. As you put into practice these teachings, it is to that extent that angers assimilating each principle, and as you assimilate each principle, these increasingly part of you ... will be made until poufs what you make of course ... And this learner is more wonderful than you will experience when you see what you've accomplished, thanks to your efforts, discipline, perseverance and perseverance ... Well remember that *"If you have any questions, you can post it on my Website "or" directly write to my mail (E-mail) ".*

MásterCoach.YlichTarazona@gmail.com
http://www.reingenieriamentalconpnl.com

If you enjoyed this workshop hypnosis, and want to "help" with your contribution, to support me to continue doing this wonderful work, which, with love, prepared for you. You can do this through the following link.

http://bit.ly/PaypalDonación
Thank you for your contribution

CHAPTER SIX: CIRCLE POWER LEVEL POWER LEVEL OF AUTHORITY OR HIGHER LEVEL (FP's)

Hello such APPRENTICE, we have reached one of the most important to learn to master hypnosis as some professional chapters. And it's increase Circle of Power and your level of Force Majeure or level of authority to a higher level (FP). These techniques and advanced knowledge will allow you to develop your hypnotic skills to the next level.

This means apprentice, that this knowledge and advanced techniques allow you to create direct and indirect orders, subjective inductions and effective suggestions for optimal and effectively in the ascending scale levels of hypnosis. gradually rising in grades HYPNOSIS ELDERLY; getting up from a circle POWER or lower force level to a higher level of authority or intermediate and higher level of hypnosis. Allowing you to literally gradually ascending from an FP0, FP1, FP2, until FP5, FP6, FP7 and above. What it entitles you to generate certain hypnotic phenomena that would otherwise be impossible cause, without prior knowledge of these advanced techniques.

This principle is one of the advanced elements most important to consider when Deepen and INDUCE HYPNOTICS STATES IN HIGHER degrees or levels of hypnosis. For this reason, I have written a complete whole chapter on this particular point, so without further ado let's begin.

In the practice of hypnosis, it has been found that each order is given to the subject (patient or participant) is the cumulative force of all inductions and earlier suggestions that have been given. This cumulative process of suggestions, inductions, direct and indirect orders, hypnotic patterns and covert commandos increase Circle of Power and your level of strength to a higher level of authority; ie a level or degree SUPERIOR most advanced hypnosis that will allow you to develop your hypnotic abilities more powerfully; whether they are in your sessions of therapeutic hypnosis or hypnosis shows your shows.

Now to continue apprentice, and deeper into this topic; the first thing I'm going to explain are the different degrees or levels of hypnosis. Grade Levels or hypnotics are known as "FP". Mastering the "FP" is allowing you to move up in your CIRCLE OF POWER or your level of strength to a higher level of authority. That is, a higher in degrees or levels of HYPNOSIS LEVEL. In other words, the "FP" is the influence you have and exert persuasive power that in actual practice, when generating orders, suggestions and hypnotic inductions.

<u>LEVELS OF GRADES or HYPNOSIS - According to (FP's)</u>

<u>FP0</u>.- It is the first degree or level of hypnosis, ie is the suggestible state in which we are at all times. You can say it is the waking state in which we are alert to any information that comes to us through the 5 senses, and we are so consciously attentive to accept or not an idea, opinion or suggestion we receive in our environment.

<u>FP1</u>.- apprentice; the degree or level "FP1" is when we begin our communication process; that is, when we started subtly convey our ideas in our conversations, opinions or suggestions, so that people with whom we come in contact begin to accept them consciously. I'll give you two (2) Examples: 1 is the most common "FP"; is the "FP1" we use every day in our conversations, allowing us to communicate our ideas, thoughts, feelings, opinions or suggestions to people or individuals with whom we come into contact and interact daily, whether these friends, acquaintances, family and even strangers. And this happens so often and unconsciously, when asked when such a complete stranger and it responds kindly, when we suggest a movie to a good friend and this access to see her happy, when we share a close a thought or a feeling and we are heard, and finally when we share an idea in a group, in our work or study center and this is received and accepted by all IDEA THE TRUTH Do you understand? That is, the "FP1" is the level or degree of hypnosis in which we influence; and which at the same time we are influenced in our daily interactions and conversations with others. - In the 2nd example, the "FP1" applies to hypnosis as such. For example, when we started our hypnotic process with a subject (patient or participant) and started to reach a level of force or positive influence on the person; so that the subject with whom we are interacting starts accessing our suggestions, allowing us to begin to give basic commands and this begins to accept our suggestions and let go voluntarily and knowingly by the inductions we give them. At this point, you can order the (patient or participant) to close his eyes, and this will. You can suggest your eyelids begin to be more and more tired and heavy; and that as deeply relaxes, and is carried away by this feeling of being his eyes began to blink more and more frequently until you feel the desire and the need to close them completely. And once they closed his eyes are so relaxed, you cannot open them. At this point, if the subject followed our instructions correctly, the person can try to open eyes, but cannot do so, since it has accepted the suggestion that they are so relaxed and stuck to them becomes normal unable to open his eyes, allowing you to dive deeper and deeper into the hypnotic state desired "FP1" and opens to be introduced to a force level to a higher level of authority. That is, to a higher level of "FP2" Now you understand the idea, right? This is what is known as CIRCLE OF POWER "FP". That is, this is the first degree or hypnotic level, the "FP1". At a higher level of "FP2" Now you understand the idea, right? This is what is known as CIRCLE OF POWER "FP". That is, this is the first degree or hypnotic level, the "FP1". At a higher level of "FP2" Now you understand the idea, right? This is what is known as CIRCLE OF POWER "FP". That is, this is the first degree or hypnotic level, the "FP1".

FP2.- Apprentice, the degree or level "FP2" is when you reach a level or degree of force to a level greater authority in hypnosis. That is, you increase your CIRCLE OF POWER or higher level of influence and persuasion on the subject, so you can instruct your subconscious mind to start moving one finger or one hand levitate. And the person in question; You can start feeling as the case or order received, either begin to feel the trembling of one of his fingers, or literally feel begins to float one hand unconsciously, only through the power of your mind Subconscious and its ability to imagine and recreate the situation that we ordered.

So this degree or level of influence and persuasion exerted on the subject, you can tell or order something like: I want you begin to notice as one of "Your fingers start to move" or a "Your hand starts to levitate "you'll notice as one of" Your fingers begin to tremble "or a" Your hands start to float "and literally if the person in question has followed our instructions previously; and has agreed to follow our orders before, it is more likely that the finger of the subject began to cause a slight tingling sensation and feel begins to move the finger, or in the case of levitation arm, began slowly feel my arm obeys to the degree to lift all alone with the power of your subconscious mind and his ability to imagine and recreate the situation.

Apprentice; insomuch its level of hyper-suggestibility, this obeys and fulfills the order received and make that subjective reality; so that, even if the subject would not move a finger or lower the arm you can no longer do, because he has already accepted the order and your mind subconsciously produced the expected effect. Which it is something that impresses greatly subjects (patients or participants) because are experiencing REAL PHENOMENON HYPNOTIC allowing you to have more control over your subconscious mind; ie it is allowing them to take greater control over himself, realizing the extent of the established order; and experience the desired "FP2" hypnotic state. This opens the door to a force level to a higher level of authority. That is to say, at a higher level of "FP3" Did you see how interesting and powerful is to understand these concepts and apply them correctly? This my friends, is what we know as CIRCLE OF POWER "FP". That is, this is the second degree or hypnotic level, "FP2".

FP3.- To continue with the above idea, we can say conclusively that the "FP3" is a higher degree of strength of a higher level of authority than the previous "FP2". That is, the "FP3" significantly increases the POWER CIRCLE GRADE LEVEL AND HIGHER Influence and Persuasion on the subject and so on You see what I mean? That as you move up in grade or level of "FP" your power of influence and persuasion exerted on the subject is also increasing, you hear well what I'm saying? By increasing your "FP" HYPNOTIC also increase your power.

FP3, FP4, FP5.- apprentice; from the degrees or levels of HYPNOSIS "FP3" "FP4" "FP5" begin to produce the greatest hypnotic phenomena. That is, in these degrees or levels of HYPNOSIS "FP3", "PF4" "FP5" is where it begins to exert greater control over the subconscious mind of the subject, and the phenomena of hypnotic trance MILD or surface Z1 occur, the HYPNOTIC TRANCE MEDIUM or cataleptic Z1-Z2 and HYPNOTIC TRANCE THRESHOLD or somnambulistic Z2. Thus, the subconscious mind of the subject begins to more easily follow orders, instructions, suggestions and inductions that gives the hypnotist.

And it is from here, my precious apprentices, where the real persuasive resources begin to occur in hypnotic communication. Since these **DEGREES** *or levels of* HYPNOSIS "FP3", "PF4" "FP5" *are who allow us to subconsciously associate a desired state of mind or state of consciousness altered an everyday occurrence, allowing the subject (patient or participant) potentially stimulate AC subjective reality helping in this way, to get answers to stimulate and develop ideo motor, ideo sensory, emotional and ideo-top at an unconscious level and cause activate your alternate reality* SUBJECTIVE; *and thus, it is much more receptive power of the subject (patient or participant) to receive the [guidance, instruction, suggestions, hypnotic suggestions, inductions and direct or indirect orders] that we are establishing.*

These degrees or levels of HYPNOSIS "FP3" "FP4" "FP5" are hypnotics processes, which are closely related to certain advanced techniques inductions and verbal suggestions strategically used by specialists, whether clinical hypnotists (hypnotherapists) or hypnotists show theater (street hypnotists), to cause certain hypnotic phenomena of higher level in the individual. As the attention of the subject (patient or participant) focuses on the power of the spoken word of the hypnotist; This eventually through verbal suggestions and hypnotic inductions is superimposed to the inner voice of the subject involved, helping to develop responses of "hyper-suggestibility", "hyper-creativity", "hyper-imagination" "hyper concentration" and "hyper-relaxation".

FP5, FP6, FP7.- (also called "HYPNOTICS Staffs") since they are considered in hypnosis as one of the degrees or higher or higher of achievable levels. Learner in these grades or levels of "FP" has managed to achieve mastery over the body and mind of the subject. And here, my dear readers where we are empowered to order the subject of a clucking like a chicken if you wanted so; and the person comply with the order without objection What interesting right? - Although logically; of course, these levels or degrees also have many other more practical and interesting applications. SUCH AS: Tibetan and Buddhist monks; use this power, degrees or levels of HYPNOSIS "FP5", "FP6" and "FP7" to give the order to walk from one city to another without getting tired. And so, their bodies go into "automatic" walking while their minds may be dreaming, thinking, or thinking about anything else. And so, their bodies arrive in perfect condition to your destination much faster than as they normally would; and also, they do without fatigue or physical fatigue, since in these states, the body remains in a total parasympathetic dominance. That is, in a "state of hyper concentration" (WAVES ALPHA / ALPHA = 8 to 13 Hz, cycles per second or cps) and a "state of rest" and "hyper-relaxation" (WAVES ZETA / THETA = 4 to 7 Hz, cycles per second or cps). Now do you understand the power you have in your hands, learning to master these degrees or levels of HYPNOSIS "FP5", "FP6" and "FP7"? their bodies arrive in perfect condition to your destination much faster than as they normally would; and also, they do without fatigue or physical fatigue, since in these states, the body remains in a total parasympathetic dominance. That is, in a "state of hyper concentration" (WAVES ALPHA / ALPHA = 8 to 13 Hz, cycles per second or cps) and a "state of rest" and "hyper-relaxation" (WAVES ZETA / THETA = 4 to 7 Hz, cycles per second or cps). Now do you understand the power you have in your hands, learning to master these degrees or levels of HYPNOSIS "FP5", "FP6" and "FP7"? their bodies arrive in perfect condition to your destination much faster than as they normally would; and also, they do without fatigue or physical fatigue, since in these states, the body remains in a total parasympathetic dominance. That is, in a "state of hyper concentration" (WAVES ALPHA / ALPHA = 8 to 13 Hz, cycles per second or cps) and a "state of rest" and "hyper-relaxation" (WAVES ZETA / THETA = 4 to 7 Hz, cycles per second or cps). Now do you understand the power you have in your hands, learning to master these degrees or levels of HYPNOSIS "FP5", "FP6" and "FP7"? since in these states, the body remains in a total parasympathetic dominance. That is, in a "state of hyper concentration" (WAVES ALPHA / ALPHA = 8 to 13 Hz, cycles per second or cps) and a "state of rest" and "hyper-relaxation" (WAVES ZETA / THETA = 4 to 7 Hz, cycles per second or cps). Now do you understand the power you have in your hands, learning to master these degrees or levels of HYPNOSIS "FP5", "FP6" and "FP7"? since in these states, the body remains in a total parasympathetic dominance. That is, in a "state of hyper concentration" (WAVES ALPHA / ALPHA = 8 to 13 Hz, cycles per second or cps) and a "state of rest" and "hyper-relaxation" (WAVES ZETA / THETA = 4 to 7 Hz, cycles per second or cps). Now do you understand the power you have in your hands, learning to master these degrees or levels of HYPNOSIS "FP5", "FP6" and "FP7"?

These degrees or levels of HYPNOSIS "FP5", "FP6" and "FP7" are ideal also to enable lucid dreaming, astral travel or try making body experiences; since these HYPNOTICS STATES or altered states of consciousness, the mind has more control over the physical and etheric body; in a way, much more transcendental, which as you would consciously in the state ALERT or wakeful state.

FP8, FP9, FP10.- (also called "HYPNOTICS STATES HIGH-LEVEL"). The following degrees or levels of HYPNOSIS "FP8", "FP9" "FP10" are what ALTERED STATES of consciousness in Schools Hypnosis is considered "impossible." Theories of degrees or levels of HYPNOSIS "FP8", "FP9" "FP10" believes and states that the hypnotic state is a real state different from the normal state monitors, unique, separately. For this reason, these hypnotic states, degrees or levels of hypnosis "FP8", "FP9" "FP10" can be created and artificially produced by the correct process of hypnotic induction, which alters the subjective experience and phenomenology of the person concerned.

Apprentice, this theory states that and reverberant CIRCLE OF POWER and levels of Force Majeure to an Authority Level or higher (FP) will allow the specialist (street hypnotist, hypnotist show, clinical hypnotist or hypnotherapist) to develop their hypnotic skills the next level; thus, limiting the critical factor in the mind of the subject (patient or participant) and altering the individual mindfulness through the suggestions and inductions that are offered up and progressively.

This theory of hypnosis levels "FP8", "FP9" "FP10" also states that there are multiple cognitive systems normally work synergistically and holistic under primary control. And, during hypnosis, normally integrated with each other, subsystems are dissociated from one another at different scales and are capable of simultaneous and independent multiple degrees of altered consciousness responses to orders, suggestions and inductions declared by the hypnotist.

DEGREES AND LEVELS OF HYPNOSIS (FP's) "continuation"

Well my precious apprentices as we have learned in the previous sections, as specialist (street hypnotist, hypnotist show clinical hypnotist or hypnotherapist) increase our circle of power, or Strength level to a higher level of authority or higher level of HYPNOSIS. We empower ourselves we literally; to go climbing or gradually rising from the FP0, FP1, FP2 levels until grades FP5, FP6, FP7 and above. This will allow us to generate certain hypnotic phenomena that are otherwise impossible cause, without prior knowledge of these advanced techniques.

That is to say; champions and champions, following the idea of the preceding paragraphs. One more specialist who is in some specialties or disciplines of hypnosis, either (street hypnotist, hypnotist show clinical hypnotist or hypnotherapist), we could get a person in the middle of the street at random, and then order him directly to be put to cluck like a chicken or send to deeply relax and sleep ... because this person probably will not! True?...

However, if the subject, either a (participant or patient) is willing to cooperate voluntarily with us in a show of hypnosis show or in a clinical hypnosis session; and you as a hypnotist, have previously followed all the above steps I've taught you, and have gradually increased Circle of Power or Strength Level to a higher level of authority at higher levels of hypnosis. It is more likely at the time that the subject in question (participant or patient), if it has shown its willingness to follow your [guidance, instruction, orders and suggestions] and you have successfully taken by the appropriate pre-hypnotic process; then, is there, at that moment my friend, that if you send them to do something simple, such as CLOSE YOUR EYES, breathing (inhale or exhale deeply) and then invite you to relax and deepen that experience, I assure you it will. Once we have achieved this first step, by earning their trust, and find ourselves as other small [hypnotic suggestions and indirect inductions] very subtle accepted gradually. The subconscious mind of the subject (participant or patient) then began to be more willing to receive our orders growing. And if at that moment we order in a very subtle way but straight to cackle like a hen that person if that will do it? Of course, it will; and the reasons why you will, is because more small order, and after accepting the above suggestions, unconsciously predisposed to accept orders greater intensity.

And if then, to continue the previous idea. Would you suggest another simple induction, then another, then another too small and simple? When you've done several of these inductions; and you've reached a good level of strength, and a good level of authority Mayor favorably. You can order you start to feel like your arm starts to levitate, and gradually feel increasingly like his arm begins to lift, gently float and levitate; Only then, his arm began to rise, float and levitate. Because already it predisposed to follow your instructions, allowing you to enter a state of hyper-suggestibility entitling him to experience these hypnotic phenomena inducing them. And then if you keep giving direct orders, subjective suggestions and inductions more or less the same level, they will fulfill each as part of a whole. And if, then, and the subject (patient or participant) is completely open to your inductions and suggestions, and tell you relax deeply and then you give the order to sleep and tell them with a subtle voice, but with authority Then that person go to sleep, if you are in the desired hypnotic state, the order is accepted by your subconscious mind, so it will! And it will fulfill your order Do you understand? the order is accepted by your subconscious mind, so it will! And it will fulfill your order Do you understand? the order is accepted by your subconscious mind, so it will! And it will fulfill your order Do you understand?

There you have all the "secret" of hypnosis. - FIRST you make the person to relax, you focus on breathing (inhalation and exhalation) and between the alpha state. Then you begin to give simple commands. At first through small inductions, but then you're making these suggestions are getting bigger. Finally, when the subject (patient or participant) delves into the hypnotic experience that you are living, you start giving orders, inductions and suggestions of a level of strength and a higher level of authority; because, your subconscious mind is ready and open to obey, so it will. You realize?

The good apprentice; It is that those orders or inductions do not necessarily have to be "direct" suggestions. Since orders, inductions and "small" suggestions can be as simple and easy to perform or continue as telling the subject to "Hearing my voice, part of your body will start to relax right now, the more things and more you concentrate on my voice, more and more you begin to feel and enjoy this state of deep relaxation, and more and more pleasant and relaxed you feel, and more and more enjoy the experience, so much so that relaxation will make you feel very nice and enter a state of hypnosis more and deeper now "have you noticed?

A KEY you have to have in mind is that: when a person enters states (WAVES ALFA / STATE = ALPHA Between 8 and 13 Hz, cycles per second or cps) body begins to relax alone. Thus, you are taking this into account; You can tell the subject in question certainly that: "As you listen to your voice, a part of your body will start to relax now," and sure there's some part of your body that has already begun to relax or and it is relaxing. So intuitively your subconscious is that part of your body that is relaxed or is relaxing; and as the subconscious is very literal (CREE that you are relaxing by the "Order of the hypnotist"). And poufs the hypnotic phenomenon begins to occur. Then when you suggest the following order "I command that relaxation is becoming more and more pleasant and enjoyable," then the subconscious (Listen to your order, notes that it is producing your prediction and feels like every time you feel more and more relaxed, and that relaxation is becoming more and more pleasant and enjoyable) and pleasurable Of course it is! Relaxation Everyone is welcome! But the subconscious does not know, and most importantly NEVER "questions the order" when transmitted correctly. So, you never think questions whether (the feeling of being aware does the person who accepts the suggestion itself), but simply the subconscious follows the order and obeys. And see, feel and perceive MULTI-sensuously that's true, that relaxation is taking place at that moment, and it is becoming more and more pleasant and enjoyable; then back again (I believe you ordered, and makes that state of relaxation increases in person) Will you understanding what I easy it is, if you do everything correctly?

Then to continue with the induction and deepen the hypnotic state desired can continue saying something like "While you relax, I command you that your breathing fence becoming more and more calm, more and more serene ever". - "Every time you inhale, you breathe more and more quietly, and so with every breath you do, make your hypnotic trance is becoming more and more deep and pleasant for you." What do you think happens when that order is given? Well, as the body is already in the states of (WAVES ALFA / STATE = ALPHA Between 8 and 13 Hz, cycles per second or cps) means that are already relaxed automatically. And when the body relaxes, breathing itself is ALWAYS more calm, relaxed, deep and serene. But as the subconscious you are listening to what you say, he thinks he is through orders that what you're giving him what he does "carry out the order" and therefore the subconscious again your orders associated with the results; and poufs the hypnotic phenomenon begins to happen again, and the subconscious (CREE that "you're in charge" that "you're giving the orders" so that the second term that "Every time you breathe, you feel COMPLY each more and more relaxed and the more and more relaxed you feel, more and more hypnotized these, and the more and more hypnotized these, more and more come in, so deep, pleasant and enjoyable deep hypnotic state as the dream itself " . what makes you feel a deep sleep, and deep sleep that induces you to sleep NOW, so sleep) Do you understand the power of suggestion? Now do you understand the power to increase and increase Circle of Power or Strength Level to a higher level of authority at higher levels of hypnosis?

As we have learned so far. The hypnotic process; and hypnotic phenomena and hyper-suggestible subconscious ability to accept orders; It is as simple as the fact properly implement the orders in the circle or power level suitable Force. Ie carry out the orders correctly in the higher levels of authority; that is, at higher levels of HYPNOSIS at appropriate times and in appropriate and more favorable circumstances for the moment Are you really agree?

How we have seen so far, my dear readers, is simple to gradually increase our circle of power, or force level to a higher level of authority at higher levels of hypnosis. So, my invitation is that you get to work, begin to take action and make things happen. And I assure you that soon you will become the best hypnotist can become. *So, without further ado let's continue with the next chapter.*

CONGRATULATIONS APPRENTICE ... WE REACHED THE END OF THIS sixth.
Now he begins learning the techniques of hypnotic inductions, covert tests, tests of suggestibility, the convincing and downriggers of hypnotic states that can make the most of, if you learn to: Increase **CIRCLE OF POWER** and your level of Force Majeure or level of authority to a higher level of (FP).

For the next chapter ...

We give some finishing touches over all the concepts and principles previously studied thus far, to make it all clear. Also apprentice, we see how a therapeutic clinical hypnosis session is to prepare and organize a show of street hypnosis or show.

Every step - by - step; to detail, not to miss anything. At the end of these chapters apprentice, you'll be in the ability to make and practice hypnosis. That is to say; "Hypnotize Anyone, Anytime, anywhere" in the circle power level of Force Majeure, level of authority and top-level (FP's) you set your mind ... since you have all the tools and knowledge necessary to become the best hypnotist can become. From henceforth apprentice, everything is in your hands, creativity, intuition and ingenuity in applying these techniques and methodologies as you see appear, according to the situations, contexts or circumstances in which you are presented your sessions of clinical hypnosis or your show events and street hypnosis show.

To test and evaluate your knowledge, you will have to do either clinical hypnosis session or prepare a show of street hypnosis, as you prefer. Ie apprentice, do real-HYPNOSIS. It will be proof for you! since they will realize the whole process in conducting a session or hypnosis show they are: (Induce, deepen, hypnotic phenomena, post-hypnotic suggestion and process of awakening) and then check the states or levels of hypnosis by what happened! and CIRCLE power level of Force Majeure, level or higher level of Authority (FP's) that have managed to achieve. So, you can assess your own progress; since, in this way, you'll know that you can correct or improve and be clear that you can rely. And if thou art something you handled properly, then ready,

As you see apprentice; It is very close so you can make a HYPNOSIS CORRECTLY. Once again, I thank you for all the interest paid in the course of practice hypnosis. ^_^

Good **LEARNERS**, THIS **It IS all for now**! We've almost reached the end of our hypnosis course Practice … wuao how time passes and as we advance enough. Apprentice, questions or if you feel there are some things we have learned, that you clarify LOVE more *(You know you can always count on me for anything; I'm your mentor, and I am here to guide you along the path to excellence in this wonderful journey to your destination … it is "one of the hypnotists BEST YOU CAN BECOME")* …
^ _ ^

If there is something that may not yet fully understand or master; quiet apprentice, as I have said before is normal. Always keep in mind that all discipline is learned precept by precept and line upon line. As you take action, and implementing these teachings is to that extent that angers assimilating each principle, and as you assimilate each principle, these increasingly part of you … will be made until poufs you perform naturally … And this apprentice; is the most wonderful thing you can experience when you see what you've accomplished, thanks to your good mood, your dedication, patience and constant persistence … Well apprentice, remember that *"If you have any questions, you can post it on my Website "or" directly write to my mail (E-mail) ".*

MásterCoach.YlichTarazona@gmail.com
http://www.reingenieriamentalconpnl.com

If you enjoyed this workshop hypnosis, and want to "help" with your contribution, to support me to continue doing this wonderful work, which, with love, prepared for you. You can do this through the following link.

http://bit.ly/PaypalDonación
Thank you for your contribution

THE ROAD TO EXCELLENCE "Alone; When you think big, when you think you can, when you have the conviction and certainty that you will achieve and you determine out of your comfort zone. And you start to persevere in your vision and mission of purpose, to achieve reach each and every one of your most cherished goals and put your plans into action firmly to go after your dreams and start believing in yourself. So is there; you started will enjoy the results have conquered your goals proposed before.
"- YLICH TARAZONA. -

CHAPTER SEVEN: HOW TO DEVELOP A HYPNOSIS SESSION OR SHOW SPECTACLE

Introduction to Chapter.

Hello such learner, we have done a great and interesting journey together in previous chapters for basic and essential elements that need to know to effectively develop hypnotic procedures. It is important that you learn to first master the tools you've learned in previous lessons, remember not to move to the next stage of this course practice hypnosis without having an absolute mastery of techniques, resources, principles and teachings precedent in prior to this chapter.

Once, having these clear recommendations, and after having carefully studied the earlier chapters, having developed and successfully carried out the exercises, and especially having implemented over and over again, all these tools, resources, basic elements, techniques, methodologies, principles and teachings in your previous sessions or presentations. Then apprentice; If so, let us continue without further ado to our next lesson.

As they have come to realize, hypnosis done well, is not such a simple process, that means, which requires that both the hypnotist (Your Apprentice), as hypnotized (the patient or participant) put much of his will. Always trying to never let a single detail to chance; and it is due to the importance of this learner, so, in this seventh chapter, we will discuss only how to perform a hypnosis session hypnosis or show correctly from the beginning to the end ...

How are you two (2) Chapter lessons are a bit long, we divide it into two parts: "Preparation" and "Hypnosis"). In this first part we will see part of the "preparation" in which two points try the "Interview" and "evidence". And since time is money, then let's start ...

The beginning of this chapter will be a summary of everything we've learned so far. It's here; where we have to use and implement everything we know, and to what we have learned and assimilated. If we remember a little, Before the HYPNOSIS (to do a short interview or talk prehypnotic) to hypnotize the subject. In this interview or talk we have:

- Clear of any MYTH that has the "Subject" (Patient or Participant)

This point is crucial and vital to start making all hypnosis. 1 must convince the hypnotized, that the hypnotist (Your Apprentice) will be able to hypnotize him. (Any myth, doubt, fear or concerns you have the person on hypnosis. If it is not resolved before the meeting or the show, literally this could bring down our previous work) To convince him, the following must be taken into account recommendations:

✓ First, we must explain to the subject "Hypnosis is a natural state of every human being; It is that hypnosis is a special altered state of consciousness in which enters Hypnotic "(voluntarily and consent) led by the suggestions of the hypnotist and inductions. In fact, you can explain that there is self-hypnosis, and that it in your own home, you can Auto-hypnotize. In this way, you do understand the person that you do not have any "supernatural magical power" alone; you have domains to techniques and methodologies that can stimulate hyper-suggestibility of the person, allowing him more receptive to the inductions, allowing achieve perform hypnotic phenomena, with guidance, guidance and instructions given by the hypnotist, YOUR APPRENTICE or ... (This would be more or less the interview or talk PRE-hypnotic that you must have to hypnotize the subject before the session or start the show.). You could also add the following lines to prepare subconscious mind of the subject in question. "I will go the steps you need to follow to get to hypnosis. So; only if you want to hypnotize you, you will enter the state of hypnosis, are you okay? If hypnosis does not work, it will depend largely on you. (To make him understand all this apprentice, eliminate resistance to believe that hypnosis is a fight between you and him ... I mean, a battle in which, if the hypnotist gets to hypnotize the subject "lost".) ... Interview or chat PRE-HYPNOTICAL you must have with the subject to hypnotize before the session or start the show.). You could also add the following lines to prepare subconscious mind of the subject in question. "I will go the steps you need to follow to get to hypnosis. So; only if you want to hypnotize you, you will enter the state of hypnosis, are you okay? If hypnosis does not work, it will depend largely on you. (To make him understand all this apprentice, eliminate resistance to believe that hypnosis is a fight between you and him ... I mean, a battle in which, if the hypnotist gets to hypnotize the subject "lost".) ... Interview or chat PRE-HYPNOTICAL you must have with the subject to hypnotize before the session or start the show.). You could also add the following lines to prepare subconscious mind of the subject in question. "I will go the steps you need to follow to get to hypnosis. So; only if you want to hypnotize you, you will enter the state of hypnosis, are you okay? If hypnosis does not work, it will depend largely on you. (To make him understand all this apprentice, eliminate resistance to believe that hypnosis is a fight between you and him ... I mean, a battle in which, if the hypnotist gets to hypnotize the subject "lost".) ... "I will go the steps you need to follow to get to hypnosis. So; only if you want to hypnotize you, you will enter the state of hypnosis, are you okay? If hypnosis does not work, it will depend largely on you. (To make him understand all this apprentice, eliminate resistance to believe that hypnosis is a fight between you and him ... I mean, a battle in which, if the hypnotist gets to hypnotize the subject "lost".) ... "I will go the steps you need to follow to get to hypnosis. So; only if you want to hypnotize you, you will enter the state of hypnosis, are you okay? If hypnosis does not work, it will depend largely on you. (To make him understand all this apprentice, eliminate resistance to believe that hypnosis is a fight between you and him ... I mean, a battle in which, if the hypnotist gets to hypnotize the subject "lost".) ...

✓ As we have discussed so far, it is important to clarify all these uncertainties that exist around hypnosis, as are: What if I do not wake up? A: The state of hypnosis is a natural state in which we daily every human being in one way or another, which tells us that hypnosis could never cause us any trouble ... I will share some examples: Imagine that a person is in through a hypnosis session, and for some reason the hypnotist had to leave urgently to solve some unforeseen, what would happen to the person? As usual would happen if you were taking a nap "wake" that is, that if a person was in a state of deep hypnotic trance, and if the hypnotist had gone just a moment and the person him want to go to the bathroom, just wake up from trance to go to the bathroom because more relaxed than a more profound person and were in a state of hypnosis, the funny thing is that when you have to go to the bathroom, be subject only automatically wake, as if he had awakened from sleep all night. Then as time, there is no problem regarding the fear of not waking up. You can do with a hypnotized person what you want, without so will? A: That will never happen, because we must remember that the person enters the state of hypnosis voluntarily and consciously driven by the suggestions and inductions declared by the hypnotist. You have to know is that, when entering hypnosis, never lose consciousness, except that you enter an altered this state; It is in a state of deeper than normal concentration. And in no time, you'll lose your consciousness or will; ie never going to do anything against your will in hypnosis, never do anything that is against our principles, morals, beliefs or ideals and morals. But, why then people behaves like a certain animal, a dog, like a cat, a chicken, etc.? ANSWER: Well; Simply because your conscious and unconscious mind sees this act as an act that at no time would be detrimental to ... I mean; when a specialist hypnotist shows a show get a subject to behave like a certain animal, and adopt the behavior of a dog, a cat or a chicken, it is simply because the subject himself unconsciously knows intuitively that it is just a role play. You see how simple? Recall that our mind has a mechanism of self-preservation, and when we find ourselves at risk, react automatically to avoid danger. If we were hypnotized and ordered us to do something against our principles, morals, beliefs or ideals and morals, our bodies react awakening from hypnosis? ANSWER: Yes; of course, yes. If in a state of hypnosis, you are commanded to imitate the dog, or act like a cat, or cackle like a chicken, and it was very inappropriate for you, I sure would not. Same with the use of hypnosis to "ask you a personal question." If you do not want to say something, or respond to a particular thing, never would, because you always have the choice and decide for yourself how far anger in hypnosis, ie hypnosis is limited, only the person does hypnosis experience unique, wonderful, special and unlimited; ie without limits, because under hypnosis everything that a person could make do with guidance, guidance and instructions of the hypnotist wants.

In short, we must make believe and do know the subject, that hypnosis will occur correctly. And you have everything under control, and they can trust you, in your experience and professionalism to make hypnosis a unique, wonderful and unforgettable experience for them.

✓ Once achieved our first step, clear the doubts ... Now in this second step, we need to get all the data about possible physical and psychological problems if any. And so, removed from our session or show any technique that works with that specific problem. (For example, if the subject (patient or participant) had heart problems, remove all techniques, for example, reduce heart rate) and psychological problems, try to avoid provoking situations to which the subject has phobia. RECALLS refrain from THERAPIES! If you do not know or do not have the qualifications, do not. We must try that hypnosis is done in the safest way possible, avoid hazardous conditions. (By nature, should enter into a risk, automatically wake up the person because of that defense mechanism we have. Anyway, and even if there is a "big" real, best to avoid situations that spoil hypnosis and confidence you have placed in us the subject risk)

Part One: HYPNOSIS SESSION according to the viewpoint of the beholder

To start, I will begin by describing how the development of a hypnosis session, from the point of view of the subject (viewer) patient or participant:

When starting the hypnosis session, most likely the subject (viewer) patient or participant at first may be that this a little distracted or focused on the expectations you have about what will or may happen. This process can begin mostly sitting, lying or standing, as applicable. Chances are that if you have some degree of experience in a previous hypnosis session will probably be relaxed and thinking normally what you should do shortly. If the contrary is your first time, you might at first feel some degree of anxiety, curiosity and have some questions regarding what you believe or think is or is not hypnosis. All these reactions or behaviors are normal, and we must keep them in mind at all times,

> *In the beginning of the hypnosis session the subject (viewer) patient or participant, it is in the NORMAL STATE OF ALERT or wakeful state (Z0). This conscious state is characterized by a high level of frequency or brain waves in neuronal activity BETA ranging from 14 to 28Hz (Cycles per second or cps)*

Once you have logged in hypnosis, the subject (viewer) patient or participant, will be in the process of transition from the normal waking state (Z0) The State HIPNOIDAL or Incantation (Z0 and Z1). Semi-conscious state, characterized by decreasing the frequency levels or brain waves in neuronal activity ALPHA / ALPHA ranging from 8 to 13*Hz* **(Cycles per second or cps)**

Once the subject (viewer) patient or participant has finished hearing the pre-hypnotic talk has responded therapeutic script, performs first tests Suggestibility, has executed some basic suggestions, you have met some orders of a CIRCLE Power or Force FP1 level and complete some orders level or higher FP2 Authority. Then the subject (viewer) patient or participant, we'll be ready to move to the next level.

To raise the subject (viewer) patient or participant to the next level and achieve our goal can do so using one of the methods most popular and effective induction, for example: Dave Elman induction model. Once achieved our purpose, the subject (viewer) patient or participant enters the next state of mild hypnotic trance Superficial Z1. This semi-conscious state, is characterized by a greater decrease in the frequency levels or brain waves in neuronal activity ZETA / THETA ranging from 6 to 7*Hz* **(Cycles per second or cps).**

In this state Z1 the subject (viewer) patient or participant knows that he is still semi-conscious. So sometimes doubt is in a state of hypnosis, and listening to the hypnotist and perceives everything that happens in their surroundings and environment around him. As this state is very unstable, and the individual always tends to return to normal waking state. For this reason, it is advisable that during this period, the hypnotist, Hypnotist, hypnotist or hypnotherapist must take into account the switch and deepen with audible, tactile and visual techniques to bring the person to the next level of hypnotic trance MEDIUM or cataleptic Z1 and Z2. This state of semi-major unconsciousness **Hz (Cycles per second or cps)** outwardly perceptible.

Now from here, it happens a very interesting fact. By increasing the circle of power, or Strength Level (FP3 and FP4), and has completed some commands authority level or higher FP5 and above. Then the subject (viewer) patient or participant, we'll be ready to move to the next higher grade advanced level.

Upon entering the subject (viewer) patient or participant in this state of deep hypnotic trance state known as somnambulistic THRESHOLD HYPNOTIC TRANCE Z2. This state is the most hypnotic trance reached, and is characterized by a greater degree in reducing the frequency levels or brain waves in neuronal activity DELTA ranging from 0.5 to 3 Hz or (cycles per second or fps), which is externally perceptible clarity compared to the previous ones.

It is important to note at this point that (By conducting covert tests, convincing and techniques deepening hypnotic states) the subject (viewer) patient or participant, began to have moments of disorientation, resulting in a temporary erase from your events perceived by your conscious mind. What will make the subject (viewer) patient or participant forget temporarily or sporadically covert tests, convincing and deepening techniques that induce hypnotic states and brought into that state of deep hypnotic trance.

Saying that he erases or forget temporarily or sporadically certain events, I mean that when I wake up the subject and return to your state of alertness (alertness or wakefulness), if we asked you to tell us everything you remember since the beginning of the hypnosis session, will remember only so far before, what brought him into the state of deep hypnotic trance.

FOR EXAMPLE: *Suppose we started giving suggestions and direct inductions your left arm will be very, very light, and when it is very light, it starts to levitate, float, rise up and unconsciously through the power of his mind. Then we accompanied him a disguised test a downrigger to give you a direct order to the left arm to bend and approaches her face slowly until the touch. Then we continue with the suggestions of a circle or power level Force (FP3 and FP4). And when we have deepened the experience and the subject (viewer) patient or participant has completed the orders of a higher level of authority or higher level FP5 and ordered to fall asleep. So, at this time,*

Then when you wake up and return to their state of alertness (alertness or wakefulness) and ask you to tell us what you remember. This will only remember your hand up. (Will forget and was erased temporarily or sporadically specific action that brought him into the state of deep hypnotic trance. That is, you forget that your left hand touches his face and fell asleep) Yes, the person knows that there is something more, but you cannot remember, when asked "what do you remember the word 'face'?" that he forgot he will come to mind and remember it perfectly ...

While the subject (viewer) patient or participant is in the THRESHOLD HYPNOTIC STATE OF TRANCE somnambulistic Z2 (deep), everything that happens not remember, unless we indicate you are to remember it.

May on rare occasions, and rarely that during the hypnosis session, the subject (viewer) patient or participant if new to hypnotic procedures, it is inexperienced or is very, very tired, exhausted, upset and He stressed for some reason; which of course it can happen. These above reasons, you can do enter the state Z3 (State Very Deep Reverie); If this phenomenon happens, you will notice very easily, seeing that the subject does not respond to our suggestions and see it even really sleep (literal or physiologically) talking. In this state Z3 (Condition Very Deep Reverie), the subject even once awakes, he cannot remember anything that has happened at this stage. (Although it reminds us) and the reason is simple and easy "It was because he fell asleep,

This is logical, and it is very clear. It's like trying to remember a sleepwalker (who speaks and walks while asleep) remember what he did or said while asleep. Is it impossible right? Well the same is true in this state Z3 (State Very Deep Reverie).

Now for covert testing, TESTING suggestibility, the convincing and deepening of state...

Both **convincing**, Suggestibility Tests, undercover tests and Downriggers Hypnotic States; are techniques of suggestion and induction, that are made subtly throughout the course of the sessions or shows, through certain methodologies used by the hypnotist wisely, to make the process of hypnosis practice easier. (In this way, we prepare the pre- we suggest the subject in his belief that hypnosis session or entertainment show will be held successfully person). That is, that is the perception that we must make him believe and experience on the subject.

These suggestion techniques and induction also serve to check the status of sugestionabilidad the subject, and to use them to produce the (desired state of hypnotic trance) and generate, hypnotic phenomena.

> **Let us sum** *One of the essential things you need to get here (During testing, the* **convincing** *and downriggers of states) is enabled on the person your HIPER-suggestibility, (ability to receive orders, suggestions and inductions) that will finally allow the subject believe, feel and experience that hypnosis is real, and it is possible to be hypnotized ...*

Today there are many **convincing***, Suggestibility Testing, Testing and Undercover Downriggers Hypnotic States. In this part of the chapter we will learn some of the most effective and efficient in generating hypnotic trance states in different degrees and levels deep ... So, without further ado apprentices continue with the lesson.*

COVERT tests, suggestibility, the convincing and deepening of state hypnotics.

Crash Test Backwards:

To begin the first thing, we do is the subject stand; with feet together and his arms loose and relaxed side. First of all, explain to the person in detail what will happen in advance (this allows us to suggesting it and preparing for what will happen) we could start by saying the following:

"Right now, you're going to stand with both feet together, and fully or partially closed eyes and relaxed. Then, then I'll put me behind you and put my hands on the side of the face up to your chest or solar plexus, and the other hand the I will place in the back, on your back on the same height as the hand forward, and keep my hands and placed in that position while doing the exercise, but without touching you. Since my hands always will be about 4 or 5 centimeters apart. Do you agree? Do you understand what we're going to do it? Yeah ... right Ok, ready continue ...

Once both placed in the correct position to begin the exercise, I will begin to speak softly, and watch as I talking to you, your body slowly began to totter. From there, once your body begins to falter, you will feel a force pushing your whole body forward and backward, feeling wobbling, swinging will be as pleasant for you, you cannot help it; and the more effort you make to keep you standing resist harder it will be. As at all times you will be aware, when you feel you're ready to let you fall, you can give me a settled with your head your ready signal. So, I will be alert to hold you to prevent you from falling. (It is important to know that will always be awake, attentive and conscious throughout the hypnotic procedure). So, when you feel it will now fall back, let yourself go, because I'll be here watching over you, so that everything goes well ... "I also want you to know that I at all times be alert and ready to exercise out properly and to hold you at all times. " I will often ask you if you agree and are ready to continue, this allows you to hear, see and feel that we are working together and you can always count on me and trust in me and in the process at all times Are you okay? SI Are you ready to start? YES. Ok ... ready ... Then start so that everything goes well ... "I also want you to know that I at all times be alert and ready to exercise properly and to hold you out at all times". I will often ask you if you agree and are ready to continue, this allows you to hear, see and feel that we are working together and you can always count on me and trust in me and in the process at all times Are you okay? SI Are you ready to start? YES. Ok ... ready ... Then start so that everything goes well ... "I also want you to know that I at all times be alert and ready to exercise properly and to hold you out at all times". I will often ask you if you agree and are ready to continue, this allows you to hear, see and feel that we are working together and you can always count on me and trust in me and in the process at all times Are you okay? SI Are you ready to start? YES. Ok ... ready ... Then start see and feel that we are working together and you can always count on me and trust in me and in the process at all times Are you okay? SI Are you ready to start? YES. Ok ... ready ... Then start see and feel that we are working together and you can always count on me and trust in me and in the process at all times Are you okay? SI Are you ready to start? YES. Ok ... ready ... Then start

<u>GETTING STARTED</u>: With the subject in a standing position with both feet together, hands on each side, loose and relaxed, with fully or partially closed eyes and relaxed. After explaining all this, we put one of our hands in front of the person at the height of the solar plexus (chest) and the other hand placed behind the subject in the back at the same height each other, about 4 or 5 centimeters without touching the person (technical MOPPAO). Once hands positioned in the correct position; without touching him, (While the hypnotist focuses on the image of the subject falling backward, as if Jan is already happening moment) we started suggest it.

<u>NOTES OF INTEREST</u>: *With Crash Test Backwards (create a situation we know the psychological consequences) we know in advance that a person who is standing with both feet together, sooner or later will make a rocking motion. So, we'll start talking a strange force that is trying to move his body. And as we know to be balanced when it does, we will tell (Sync through suggestion): "! You see Already start* *movements" This is essential "This way we make your unconscious believe everything you say then comes this strange force. (If we told him that a strange force would begin to swing it, now that you say that your body feels strongly pushed back, unconsciously believe that feels pushed back and inevitably will fall back.) In this suggestion is based. Believe and feel to give the person to be produced and is producing something (we all know that will occur). By the fact that the hypnotist says and takes place, the subconscious accepts it receives as it was the hypnotist who produced it through his words. So, from then on, anything you say the hypnotist will occur as well. (To get hypnosis, we see that we need to go into thinking, feeling and experiencing the subject gradually hypnosis has taken over your body) finally inducing the desired state we want (Divert suggestion to the marked target) in this case, it would fall back,*

To achieve this goal, we say: From the moment I want you to focus on your whole body, just now begin to feel a very strange feeling, soon, you'll notice that your body sways and feel like your body slowly starts moving gently forward and backward, you feel like those little movements are increasing more and more, you feel like an alien force balance begin gently forward and backward. And I want you when you start to feel that sense of swing, you focus on the experience you are living and experiencing your body and feel that strange force begins to move and balance your body. " That's right, you're doing very well, and started to wobble perfect.

REMEMBER: *You have to talk to the person in the present tense, as if he were producing and verifying the hypnotic phenomenon at that moment.*

very important part *If you see you are not having the expected results, quiet, relax, it's normal, it can happen that the person needs more time and suggestion. To help you regain control of the situation, try to change the volume, tempo, rhythm and tone of voice; and adapt it to the situation, the context and the circumstances that are living also incorporating your body language, verbal and nonverbal, as we learned in previous lessons.*

(Once the subject does some small movement, make you believe, feel and experience that this movement has been caused by the "strange force")
"You see, you felt that? Your body has moved ... From now on, the strange force takes control of your body, and begins gently wobble more and more and push you forward and backward. You cannot go longer standing. That strange feeling of wellbeing is stronger than you. The movements are becoming more and more intense, and you may notice the right?

(Continues until fall. The normal for a person to fall time are 2, 3 and 5 minutes) (Warning! ... There are also people who fall at 10 and 30 seconds! ... so, every time you have to be alert, ready and prepared to hold early and prevent it from falling out.)

This test of suggestibility always works 90% of the time, with high probability of success, if we are careful and pay attention to any movement that makes the person, and make him believe, feel and experience in the subject's mind that this movement has been infused by that strange force.

Test lock eyeballs, eyelids heavy or Catalepsy Eye:

Blocking techniques of eye, eyelids or catalepsy Heavy Eye balloons is founded on two (2) METHODOLOGIES.
"1 Physiological" organ function or body's natural response
"2nd Suggestible " Inductive Response Suggestibility or Psychological

1. - LOCK Eyeballs -Eyes glued (PHYSIOLOGICAL)

This 1st technique of suggestion and induction of catalepsy eye, is a "test Suggestibility" which has a strong physiological component, (organ function or body's natural response), which will help us in our process of "Pre-Election / prehypnotic "to prepare and select the subject (patient or participant) with whom we will work in our sessions or hypnosis shows. If this technique of suggestion and induction of catalepsy eye is performed correctly, it will allow us to achieve three things:

1 suggestible properly preselect the candidate with whom we will start working on our therapeutic clinical hypnosis sessions or at our shows of street hypnosis or show.

2Subtly rid of people who are not interested in actually participating in our clinical sessions or hypnosis show; or prevent and detect those who try to challenge us, or are simply not yet ready to be hypnotized, but perhaps later be motivated to participate.

3 mentally prepare the subject with whom we will work, earn their trust, get into rapport with him, generate empathy and encourage you to participate actively and willingly, with an intention of positive purpose, which allows us to have an excellent session of therapeutic hypnosis or make a good show of show.

Yes, in September: *A technique used to get put the subject on our side, and who agrees with us at least 3 "YES" followed ("covert orders").*

FOR EXAMPLE: *You can sit / stand "Yes", you can raise your legs / feet "Yes", you can take a deep breath "Yes". From that moment, it will be much simpler than your subconscious mind accesses our suggestions and inductions more freely, so it is ready to start the hypnotic process.*

The steps then apply Yes in September are as follows:

Step 1: *I want you to relax, take a deep breath, inhales and exhales, Inhale - Exhale, Inhale - Exhale. So is; right, you're doing fine. Now I want you to focus, and follow my finger I'll go pulling him slowly, more and more the center of your two eyes (eyebrows). Now you begin to notice how your eyes clouds, notice how your vision becomes more and more blurred, and you begin to have a slight feeling of heaviness* *in the eyelids and feel the desire to close my eyes. I feel that when those things; completely close your eyes, relax your eyelids completely and you stay deeply relaxed. Perfect; so, very well. Now with eyes closed, I want you to imagine that you can see over your forehead, here in this part where I'm playing with the tip of my finger (Place finger and make some pressure in the middle of his forehead "Frown" up to the "Third Eye"). "We must always keep the subject under suggestion at all times saying" I want you to imagine now; even keeping your eyes closed, your forehead is a window; and you can see out, imagine that your forehead is transparent or translucent, and you can see my finger, and follow his path, even with your eyes closed, you can see and follow the path of my finger ... Great, you're doing fine.*

__Step 2__: That's right, now I will go up a little more and more finger slowly across your forehead to above your head, and I want to follow the path my finger with your eyes fully closed; That's fine. Continues displaying focused on my finger; follow its trajectory; Look at him, follow him, right, so, fine. Now I want you to look up, up to where my finger (Place your finger and make some downward pressure on the center top of his head). "We must continue to keep the person under suggestion at all times ordering him to" imagine that you can see not only my finger, but also the (roof, clouds, trees, etc.) across your forehead, as if it were an open window in your head that allows you to see even the outside with closed eyes. That's; Excellent, you're doing fine.

__Step 3__Have great difficulty doing ... Your eyes are completely sealed, fully glued ... Your eyelids can no longer be lifted and, at times, despite all your efforts, it will be impossible to open your eyes ... Muscles constrict your eyes ... the more time passes, more solidly stick your eyelids ... When I count to "three" your eyelids and your eyes will be completely closed, merged, joined and sealed ... As much as you strain to lift your eyelids, not make it ... as I say "three" will be impossible to open your eyes ... One 1 ... your eyes are firmly closed ... Two 2 ... your eyelids are getting more and tighter ... THREE! Your eyelids are held together and completely stuck, your eyes are totally sealed and fused ... Your eyes are completely sealed, fully glued ... your eyelids and cannot be lifted and, at times, despite all your efforts, it will be impossible to open your eyes ... your eyes muscles contract ... the more time passes, more solidly stick your eyelids ... When I count to "three" your eyelids and your eyes will be completely closed, merged, joined and sealed ... as much as you try to lift your eyelids, not as you will achieve ... I say "three" will be impossible to open your eyes ... One 1 ... Your eyes are firmly closed ... Two 2 ... Your eyelids are getting more and more crowded ... THREE! Your eyelids are held together and completely stuck, your eyes are totally sealed and fused ... Your eyes are completely sealed, fully glued ... your eyelids and cannot be lifted and, at times, despite all your efforts, it will be impossible to open your eyes ... your eyes muscles contract ... the more time passes, more solidly stick your eyelids ... When I count to "three" your eyelids and your eyes will be completely closed, merged, joined and sealed ... as much as you try to lift your eyelids, not as you will achieve ... I say "three" will be impossible to open your eyes ... One 1 ... Your eyes are firmly closed ... Two 2 ... Your eyelids are getting more and more crowded ... THREE! Your eyelids are held together and completely stuck, your eyes are totally sealed and fused ... Your *eyelids can no longer be lifted and, at times, despite all your efforts, it will be impossible to open your eyes ... your eyes muscles contract ... The more time passes, more solidly your eyelids stick ... When I count to "three" your eyelids and your eyes will be completely closed, merged, joined and sealed ... for more than hard you to raise your eyelids, you will not make it ... as I say "three" you will find it impossible to open eyes ... One 1 ... Your eyes are firmly closed ... Two 2 ... Your eyelids are getting more and more crowded ... THREE! Your eyelids are held together and completely stuck, your eyes are totally sealed and fused ... Your eyelids can no longer be lifted and, at times, despite all your efforts, it will be impossible to open your eyes ... your eyes muscles contract ... The more time passes, more solidly your eyelids stick ... When I count to "three" your eyelids and your eyes will be completely closed, merged, joined and sealed ... for more than hard you to raise your eyelids, you will not make it ... as I say "three" you will find it impossible to open eyes ... One 1 ... Your eyes are firmly closed ... Two 2 ... Your eyelids are getting more and more crowded ... THREE! Your eyelids are held together and completely stuck, your eyes are totally sealed and fused ... Your eye muscles contract ... The more time passes, more solidly stick your eyelids ... When I count to "three" your eyelids and your eyes will be completely closed, merged, joined and sealed ... For more that you strive to raise your eyelids, you will not make it ... as I say "three" will be impossible to open your eyes ... One 1 ... your eyes are firmly closed ... Two 2 ... your eyelids are becoming more and tighter ... THREE! Your eyelids are held together and completely stuck, your eyes are totally sealed and fused ... Your eye muscles contract ... The more time passes, more solidly stick your eyelids ... When I count to "three" your eyelids and your eyes will be completely closed, merged, joined and sealed ... For more that you strive to raise your eyelids, you will not make it ... as I say "three" will be impossible to open your eyes ... One 1 ... your eyes are firmly closed ... Two 2 ... your eyelids are becoming more and tighter ... THREE! Your eyelids are held together and completely stuck, your eyes are totally sealed and fused ... For more than hard you to raise your eyelids, you will not make it ... As I say "three" will be impossible to open your eyes ... One 1 ... Your eyes are firmly closed ... Two 2 ... your eyelids are getting more and more crowded ... THREE! Your eyelids are held together and completely stuck, your eyes are totally sealed and fused ... For more than hard you to raise your eyelids, you will not make it ... As I say "three" will be impossible to open your eyes ... One 1 ... Your eyes are firmly closed ... Two 2 ... your eyelids are getting more and more crowded ... THREE! Your eyelids are held together and completely stuck, your eyes are totally sealed and fused ...*

_step 4_*Now, I want you to try to open my eyes, without forcing anything, do it naturally and see that, for a few seconds, you cannot open them, you will feel like you are stuck alone for a few moments, you will see that it is impossible to open normally, and the more you try, more and more are stuck, and the more you try to open them gently, more and more will be sealed to such an extent that you cannot open them ... that's right, without forcing anything, well right, you're making. Now stop trying, (not let them try too, with a couple of seconds worth, as a little dizzy and very uncomfortable) that is; CHILL OUT NOW again and stop trying, but keep your eyes closed. That's; excellent, you did very well. (Lower the finger to the height of the eyebrows.)*

_step 5_*Now relax your eyelids, I want you to relax your eyes, that's, now take a deep breath, relax and get back to Inhaling and exhaling, Inhale - Exhale, Inhale - Exhale. So is; OK, you did very well, you can open your eyes very relaxed feeling them. You can open your eyes slowly ... That's right, very right, congratulations you did very well ... ^ _ ^*

It seems a simple and easy exercise; and it is, if performed correctly and applied, and, above all, an amazing response causes many people. That apprentice is good, as it predisposes to continue the session or participate more in the show.

2. - LOCK Eyeballs -Eyes glued (SUGGESTION)

This 2nd technique of suggestion and induction of catalepsy eye, is a "test Suggestibility" which has a strong psychological component stimulation (Hiper-Suggestibility and Response Inductive) of the person, action to help us in our process "Pre-Election / prehypnotic" to prepare and select the subject (patient or participant) with whom we will work in our sessions or hypnosis shows. This technique of suggestion and induction is very useful to check if the person is ready to work or not; while it is allowing us like the previous one, achieving three major purposes: (Remember).

1 suggestible properly preselect the candidate with whom we will start working on our therapeutic clinical hypnosis sessions or at our shows of street hypnosis or show.

2Subtly rid of people who are not interested in actually participating in our clinical sessions or hypnosis show; or prevent and detect those who try to challenge us, or are simply not yet ready to be hypnotized, but perhaps later be motivated to participate.

3 mentally prepare the subject with whom we will work, earn their trust, get into rapport with him, generate empathy and encourage you to participate actively and willingly, with an intention of positive purpose, which allows us to have an excellent session of therapeutic hypnosis or make a good show of show.

> *Yes, in September*: *You can sit / stand "Yes", you can raise your legs / feet "Yes", you can take a deep breath "Yes".*

The steps then apply Yes in September are as follows:

Step 1: *I want you to relax, take a deep breath, inhales and exhales, Inhale - Exhale, Inhale - Exhale. So is; right, you're doing fine. Now I want you to take another deep breath; but this time, releasing the air, I want you to look a bit down, in a position of your head that you are and you feel comfortable and let your eyes close completely, press them tightly, also close your eyelids tightly, you have pressure your eyes and eyelids to stick together completely, again lobbying to join and fully merge, and let your eyelids and your eyes close completely, totally. Perfect; That's right, you're doing very well.*

Step 2 *Now relax, breathe deeply again, inhales and exhales, Inhale - Exhale, Inhale - Exhale. Quite so! you are doing it very well. Now I want you to imagine all the muscles around your eyes relax completely, I want you to allow yourself to feel your relaxed eyelids, allow yourself to feel the muscles above your eyes relaxed, the muscles under more relaxed, the muscles of the sides completely relaxed (As we say these inductions, we touch soft and subtly every part of the eye that we want the person relax (This allows the subject to remain concentrated and focused on the exercised; the same time we anchor them through touch "kinesthetic "the feeling of relaxation that we want to generate)),* To follow the suggestion will continue to say: I want you to imagine now, as would be the muscles of your eyes so relaxed that just your eyes closed and feel your eyelids are completely closed, deeply closed, completely closed, only for a short time. That is, you're doing very well.

Step 3 *Now I want you to relax completely still, these muscles of your eyes, feel them completely relaxed, totally relaxed, deeply relaxed. (As we say these inductions, soft and subtle touch every part of the eye that we want the person relax).* Have great difficulty doing ... Your eyes are completely sealed, your eyelids are completely stuck ... Your eyelids can no longer raise your eyes and cannot be opened and, at times, despite all your efforts, will be impossible to raise your eyelids open and will be impossible for you to open your eyes ... Allow yourself to feel the muscles in your eyes constrict ... the more time passes more firmly stick your eyelids ... FROM NOW, When I say "three" your eyelids and your eyes will be completely closed ... as much as you strain yourself in lift, you will not make it ... as I say "three" will be impossible to open your eyes ... One 1. Your eyes are firmly closed ... Two 2 ... Your eyelids are getting more and more crowded ... THREE! Your eyelids remain stuck,

step 4 *Now I want you when you're absolutely sure that your eyes and your eyelids are completely sealed and fully fused, I want you to imagine that you try to open them but you cannot do it, imagine it's impossible, because the feeling of contraction in your eyes eyelid is so strong, you feel your eyes and eyelids completely sealed and totally enclosed, it makes you so natural, you decide to leave your eyes closed, feeling of*

contraction is so strong that choose in your mind to keep your completely sealed eyelids and fully closed. That's right, right well, still imagining ... Now I want you even more when you are absolutely sure that your eyes and eyelids are fully bonded and fully closed, sealed and fused try to open them, but this time, simply it will be impossible to open, even if you try. That is, I want you to enjoy the feeling of not being able to open my eyes, I want you to feel your eyelids keep cone and stuck closed only for a few seconds. Try to open your eyes, but it is impossible because they are completely stuck, try to open your eyes, and the more you try, it is even more impossible to open them because they are completely closed and glued, they are completely sealed and fused. That's right, very right, congratulations you did very well ... and the more you try, it is even more impossible to open them because they are completely closed and glued, they are completely sealed and fused. That's right, very right, congratulations you did very well ... and the more you try, it is even more impossible to open them because they are completely closed and glued, they are completely sealed and fused. That's right, very right, congratulations you did very well
...^ _ ^ Now to be able to open your eyes and come back, count to three. To count to three, you can open your eyes ... One 1 your eyelids relax ... Two begin to open your eyes ... THREE 3! You can open your eyes! Open them NOW ...

__NOTE OF INTEREST__ Here, in the "Test Suggestibility" of catalepsy Eye or (Lock Eyeballs - eyes glued, it may happen that: The person open your eyes; if so, it is just okay we ask kindly to close eyes again, and relax all your muscles, you say "close your eyes and make sure this time that all the muscles around your eyes are completely relaxed, deeply relaxed, totally relaxed ...

Suggesting it still subtly and through inductions and say emphatically that covert orders and directly: Only you can do it, it's in you, achieve imagine until it happens; I cannot do it for you "but you if you can, I know you can do it, try again (and repeat the question of compromise -" When you're absolutely sure that your eyes would not open, try again and allow yourself to discover it is impossible. "the second time, returning to repeat the exercise, if the person followed all your instructions, and allowed himself to be carried away by the experience, it is almost certain and sure that in 90% to 95% of cases, which if this time work.

IMPORTANT And if, for some reason, will not work, quiet, just we have to work on the unconscious resistance you may have the individual. Thank you, politely dismiss him, and invite him to participate in another opportunity. Since people (patients or participants) who resist the test of suggestibility, also probably unconsciously resist the inductive act of other inductions because they demonstrate that they are unable to follow the instructions that are given. This inability; It may also be unintentional and unconscious, but in any case, is a sign of resistance. And it is wiser to stop keep insisting that person, and maybe at that time is not ready, but another possible opportunity, perhaps more receptive to participate.

How could you appreciate apprentice; these two (2) different techniques physiological and psychological suggestion induction, are both "Test Suggestibility" applied in two (2) different contexts; but ultimately, they have the same goal. And the purpose of both methods is the degree of suggestibility see people and their commitment to participate actively and willingly in our sessions or shows, with all the possible arrangement.

Explanation of the Test Lock Eyeballs - Eyes glued "Catalepsy Eye (physiological)"

Actually, it's "Test Suggestibility" Lock Ocular - Eye Glued or Catalepsy in function (physiological) is not hypnosis itself. I will explain what I mean; these techniques of suggestion and physiological induction is rather a subtle to assess the degree of suggestibility of the subject trick, and at the same time it serves to convince the person of their ability to hypnotizing.

And so, to create you this idea, and implanting in his mind this belief, it is much easier, you can easily soak in the desired hypnotic trance state. Indeed, it is "Test Suggestibility" Lock Ocular - Eye Glued or catalepsy Eye on its function (Physiological) is itself an obvious physiological factor artificially recreate to generate a response, which we know physiologically will occur.

WHY DOES THIS HAPPEN? *Why; it is impossible to keep looking up eyeballs, while trying to open eyes in that position, because it is not natural for sight-seeing upward, while watching normally. For that reason; It agrees that, at the end of induction, placing the eyes of the subject (patient or participant) back into normal position, to break, muscle blockade was established with the suggestion, and so getting the person, you can open the eyelids usually again without any discomfort, and wake up with the desire to continue participating.*

("Warning! Abstaining from this test to people who wear lenses (lenses or eyeglasses) without removing them briefly, or you can give them panic unable to open your eyes! (All these risks can be avoided if ante session or show, first we assess the situation beforehand and ask the person if he agrees with the exercise that we will do)")

RECAP, FINAL AND VARIATION OF COUNCILS TECHNIQUE

• Before starting the "Test Suggestibility" Lock Ocular - Eye Glued (short version), we must first explain the subject: "This test is to close your eyes, then I'll put one of my fingers in the center of your forehead and you will look to the point where you're playing you do you agree? The duration of the test, do not take your attention to that point where I'm playing. I begin to speak, and then when you say that you cannot open my eyes; while looking to the point, make a small attempt to open them. When you see that you cannot open them, stop trying, do me a hand gesture, and I will make the can open again. "

- Lock this test we will Ocular - Eyes glued in (short version) only to the part where it says "... it is impossible to open them; You cannot open my eyes; you cannot, are closed. " Then we will say: Has an attempt to open them and see that you cannot open them. IMPORTANT (Note well the subject's eyes) (It is possible that the subject open your eyes. If so, you will notice that when you open them, you'll notice that she was not really looking up. (We know that if we had listened, and I had been looking up, would not have been able to get open eyes. (this is a secret)) in this case, we thank you for participating, and then say goodbye politely to the subject. (Perhaps another time and another voice, you test eyes closed) function.

- If you cannot open: "Excellent Apprentice" That means we achieved our goal; and that the subject unable to do the exercise correctly and followed all our instructions and is ready to move to the next level. At that time then it means that we are in charge, and that we in control. Once achieved the expected purpose, we say "See? You cannot open them! Now stop trying and keep watching the point "now your finger down slowly until again reach the starting point at the tip of his nose. "Now when I count to three, you will see like you can open your eyes. One 1 your eyes begin to peel off two 2 your eyelids begin to open three 3 Open your eyes! "And voila, the exercise is complete. We thank the person for participating,

- *You should never abuse the "Test Suggestibility" Lock Ocular - Eyes Glued or Catalepsy Eye, we know that always works, 90% of the time, if you meet the right steps, but if you are an apprentice, I advise you better use the technique induction of the "fall back". - Importantly ("Proof of Suggestibility" FALL BACK is much easier to perform and results in a 99.9% greater chance of success, better than catalepsy eye (ocular lock) in most cases, all requiring "proof fall back" is a little practice).*

The test Suggestibility "and suggestion techniques and induction relative value and variable when it comes to determine and evaluate whether a subject (patient or Participant) has a predisposition or degree (Hiper-Suggestibility) to be easily hypnotized.

Since it has been proven time and again that the tendency of one individual toward hypnosis is not constant or discontinuous, and may even vary from one day to another. Therefore, cannot be considered surprising that the result of any test Suggestibility "suggestion techniques or methodologies practiced induction a person at a given moment is negative and that; at another time, at another time and in a different circumstance, that person achieves get in a state of hypnosis without difficulty in another context or more favorable situation. Even with the same test carried out in later days.

Then we can reaffirm that: The effectiveness of the tests are really highlights; but only when it comes to measuring the depth of hypnotic trance state that applies only to that particular moment.

Test Arm Levitation "Part 1"

Test technique Arm Levitation, this methodology founded on the Inductive Response Suggestibility or Psychological.

1. - TEST ARM Levitation (SUGGESTION)

This suggestion 1 and induction technique is a deeper of hypnotic states and a disguised test according to the purpose it is made. In the downrigger Test Arm levitation subject (patient or participant) remains either sitting or lying as occasion required; against the hypnotist; he stares into his eyes, as he says:

Preparation: I want you to relax, to breathe deeply, inhale and slowly Exhale, Inhale "{leaves a second air in your lungs}" - Exhale "{release the tension and the air slowly}" Inhale "{again feel as every breath you are filled welfare, peace and a state of deep tranquility} "- exhale" {exhale and feel as with every single breath all the tension and all the stress from your body} "That's right; right, you're doing fine.

Step 1 Now I want you to concentrate and feel your left arm begins to relax, I want you to imagine as your left arm relaxes, begins to lighter and lighter, lighter and lighter, that, fine. Now I want you to focus on that feeling of relaxation and lightness in which is your left arm (every time you repeat the word left arm, touching the arm of the subject, and make a little contact kinesthetic, to accustom the person to contact you, always subtly and always maintaining suggestion, you tell him) and feel that sense of relaxation and levity every time it has been more and more pleasant. That's right, right, you're doing fine ...

Step 2: Now he wants you begin to imagine and feel your left arm (you have contact) gently begins to lift, and as you focus on that image in your mind and that feeling of levitation of your left hand (you have contact), I want notes that begins to lift as slowly as if floating or levitating started up more and more. That, very well, and began to move, feels like and began to rise and levitate. Now I want you to notice how your left arm (contact, touch up as implying that the arm has already begun to rise and levitate) begins to rise more and more, and as you relax and concentrate on that feeling of relaxation and lightness your left arm (contact you) rises, and rises more and more,

Step 3 Now feel your left arm (contact you) begins to levitate and float up toward your face. That's right, once as already started up more and more. Now allow yourself to feel your hand rises more and more towards your face, I want you to feel like your hand starts to levitate and float all the way up to your face ... Now, you know it, your arm will begin moving further and closer to your face, that is, you see how your left arm is raised (you have contact) slowly towards your face ... Now I feel like your arm starts to rise and float increasingly to the height of your face ...

step 4 Now imagine you're at a children's party, or in a very beautiful place where there are lots and lots of multicolored balloons, helium, those that float and levitate in the air and go up to heaven, so, I want you to imagine how you tie your left wrist (you have contact) hundreds and thousands of multicolored balloons, filled with helium ready to fly and float through the air, and ascend into heaven ... okay, that's, you're doing well, now I want you to let feel like those hundreds and thousands of multicolored balloons floating pull up and begin to raise your left arm (you contact, touch bottom up as insinuating that the arm has already begun to rise and levitate) more and more into the sky .. . Now imagine that all these colorful floating balloons tied to your wrist do raise your hand and raise your arm over and above feels like helium filled balloons fly very high and pull your arm up each of more and more ... Allow yourself to feel like balloons go up, and your left arm (contact you) also raised up by these beautiful multicolored balloons, so, you're doing extremely well.

step 5 *Now I want you to feel like your left arm is raised (you have contact) ... rises more and more (you have contact) ... The other arm remains stationary, but the balloon rises, rises, rises higher and higher ... feel your left arm as light as a balloon note as your left arm rises only (you have contact), more and higher ... it rises ... it rises ... continues to rise ... each higher and higher, the balloons go up, raise your arm as the rise, balloons your arm also rises inevitably ... Light like a balloon, your arm up ... up ... up ...*

END OF YEAR

Important point *This technique of suggestion is a downrigger and induction of hypnotic states, as well as covert as the purpose test to be performed. FOR EXAMPLE: If you use it as a disguised test, then you can apply this exercise unforeseen half way hypnosis session; or half of the show, to evaluate and detect the degree of suggestibility in the subject (patient or participant) is. And correctly determine the degree of hypnotic trance or hypnosis level that this person ... If at the end of the year; the person responded well to suggestions and raise my arm, to the extent that we would Suggestion was, step by step, then it means that it is likely that the subject (patient or participant) is in the state Z1, which allow us to deepen the exercise and introduce it into the Z2 state ... Did you see how important are the Covert Vinnie and used? In the second case, for example: If you use it as some downrigger United hypnotics; then, to find that the person responded well to exercise, which has its fully raised hand, and that is deeply relaxed state Z1, then we could continue with two more steps ... In this case it would be Step 6 and Step 7; and would continue as follows, to deepen the hypnotic state and introduce more fully in the Z2 state. to verify that the person responded well to exercise, which has its fully raised hand, and that is deeply relaxed state Z1, then we could continue with two more steps ... In this case it would be Step 6 and Step 7; and would continue as follows, to deepen the hypnotic state and introduce more fully in the Z2 state. to verify that the person responded well to exercise, which has its fully raised hand, and that is deeply relaxed state Z1, then we could continue with two more steps ... In this case it would be Step 6 and Step 7; and would continue as follows, to deepen the hypnotic state and introduce more fully in the Z2 state.*

step 6 *Now I want you to feel like your left arm (you have contact) rises and goes straight to your face slowly and touch your face ... The other arm remains stationary, but the left arm (you have contact) rises higher and higher towards your face until finally touches your face ... that is, you're doing very well.*

step 7 *Now notice how your left arm (contact you) begins to levitate and float up toward your face and gently touches your face. That's right, once as and your hand is near your face and subtly caressing your face (you touch, touches his hand with a finger and Draw it gently to your face insinuating that hand and began stroking his face, always subtle and always keeping the suggestion that now you order and tell). Now allow yourself to feel as you gently feel the sensation in your face fingers of your hands gently caress your face, comes more and more into a deep hypnotic trance state … (Here you approach the person and begin to rock her, moving slightly from side to the other, or back and forth, to stimulate the feeling of deep relaxation and generate the "State of Trance Hypnotic Desire) and you order saying Now, you walk into a deep sleep, sleep more and more deeply, you slip deeper and deeper into a deep hypnotic sleep … Now when I count to three you will relax even more, and you will sleep deeper and deeper still. 1 lose yourself relax 2, 3 sleep feels, now sleep!*

Recommendations and final words.

To achieve better results, it is best to keep trying all the voices have been learning; until we begin to notice favorable and positive results, and the tone or volume of voice that suits are that we should use to stimulate the desired hypnotic trance states)

If for some reason did not come out as expected, quiet, take it easy, learn from the situation, and try again, but this time, help the subject (patient or participant) make you believe that any small movement to occur in your arm, is indicative that it is very light and, for that reason, it will go up. And if you're going to deepen the state, and associate him feel the person when you touch your face goes deeper and deeper into a state of trance further and deeper … And ready^ _ ^

Test Arm Levitation "2nd Part"

To continue we will perform the same technique Test Arm levitation; but this time grounded in sensory methodology FAMILY.

TEST ARM Levitation (Family Sensorial) EXPLANATION

✓ **Create a situation in which the psychological consequences are known:** Make the subject levitation observe the movement of his left hand. (If we say we will move and levitate, the subject will be attentive to see if it moves and begins to rise. Because of this, any move you make, whatever small, will cause the subject begins to believe and feel what He tells the hypnotist, and by suggestion (covert orders), movements will become more elevated each time, until finally the lift arm)

✓ **Sync via suggestion:** We believe and feel the subject, those little movements you make, it's because the arm started to levitate, because the hand is very light, and the arm is completely and totally relaxed, allowing you to upload and levitate arm up alone.

✓   **Divert suggestion to the desired goal:** We believe and feel the subject's hand is now directed towards the face, because it has very sleepy and when the hand touch her face into a state of trance further and deeper than it is at that time. (For this reason, his hand is getting closer to the face, "false motive, but his subconscious accepts it as true").

In fact; in particular it is one of the techniques that, to me, the more I like to do, because at every moment, lets me know to what degree or level of hypnosis the subject with whom I am working is. (Person, who of course, we'll make you believe and feel that the movement of levitation of his left hand up, is because it is becoming more and lighter his arm and wants to climb up and levitate alone) Now maybe you're wondering ...

Good and What kind of person should I look for this technique? Would you work this technique a person to choose between public? Quiet apprentice, you must relax and rely on this test, the series of overlapping suggestions vary very slightly from one person to another. But above all, and most importantly, they never cast doubt on the subject at any time. (. [Since, who really will work is with the unconscious mind of the person] With this kind of test there will never be any distinction between a person who is very clever or not [Since who actually negotiated is with the subconscious mind])

So, without further ado for now, let's continue.

First of all, apprentice, we must first explain to the subject (patient or participant) everything that will happen in advance, to predispose to what will happen next, and so suggest it unconsciously, so let's not unexpected surprises: We can start the test saying:

You'll relax deeply and as you speak, you feel like your left hand will be done so but so light they begin to feel that rises alone up and begins to levitate in the air "

<u>IMPORTANT</u>*: What you should never tell the subject; It's business, which (When his hand touched her face, sleep!) and that action we realize it and make it long after ... I will briefly explain why you should avoid telling that from the beginning because if you give that from the beginning, the safest thing is that the person unconsciously throughout hypnosis would be waiting for that moment to arrive to see what happens, and hypnosis may not work as we would like, because the person would be distracted by that action.*

Already now you understand why we should not say anything? That is, only our secret, and (AS under sleeve) to deepen the subject on a deeper, at the end of the test) hypnosis. This order that your hand will touch your face, we say only near the end of the test, when the person is already completely submerged in the Z1 state (When we, through calibration (Attentive observation) see your unconscious will accept our suggestions "covert orders") required throughout the process of hypnosis. That's summit at that time, the person is more suggestible and ready to enter the state Z2, we will give you a direct order, that (When his hand touched her face, sleep!). So that's apprentice, who will be well absorbed by your subconscious ... and poufs think he will sleep.

The most recognized and famous hypnotist's world experts describe this method as one of the techniques that require a lot more patience on the part of the hypnotist; so, apprentice Let us be filled with patience and start.

2 Levitation TEST ARMS (Family Sensorial)

The hypnotist speaks to the subject of this: (It is assumed that the subject (patient or participant) to hypnotize begins first with eyes open in due course, it will give you suggestion (order) for the closing.).

Preparation: I want you to sit quietly in this chair (whether to be seated) or we can do it standing too, in either case to say I want you to relax, to breathe deeply, inhale and slowly Exhale, Inhale "{leaves a second air in your lungs}" - Exhale "{release tension and air slowly} "Inhale" {again feel like with every breath you are filled with well-being, inner peace and a state of deep tranquility} "- exhale" {exhale and feel as with every single breath all the tension and all the stress from your body} "That's right; right, you're doing fine.

Step 1Now I want once (sitting or standing as you) when you're comfortable, put your hands relaxed at his sides, sideways, loosen palms down. Okay, so it is. Now look at your left-hand concentrate on it, I want you to put all your focus and your attention on your left hand, carefully watch it. All you have to do is be (sitting or standing) and deeply relax. Then you notice that along relaxation several things happen. These things usually happen when one relaxes, but still you have not noticed what happens in your left arm, and I'm going to be noted. "

Step intermediate between 1 and step 2After a pause of a few seconds, maintaining direct contact with the subject, waiting for the person awareness your words and (Start relax) according to your instructions and unconsciously (and start thinking, what will happen and how it will happen). In those brief moments, keeping the previous step sequence say ...

Step 2"Now I want you to concentrate attentively in all the feelings you have and let you begin to feel the quality sensations in your left hand. You may notice a slight movement, very soft and subtle almost imperceptible you start to feel your left arm, or perhaps with your notes as controlled breathing, you begin to relax even more and more. Or maybe you feel as your heart beats, your relaxation is becoming more and more relaxed. Perhaps you begin to feel like your left hand, you begin to feel a sense was tingling or tingling, which tells you that already began to rise and levitate slowly. No matter what feelings notes, what I observe is that the feel and listen to your interior. Okay, that's, you're doing perfect ... Now you keep looking at your left hand, and allow yourself to realize as has begun to levitate and rise gently and slowly upward. Continues to look your left arm. Soon you'll notice a movement of more and more noticeable levitation that makes up your hand slowly ... There is movement, but has not yet note. Maybe your eyes do not perceive it, but return to carefully check your right arm, and will continue wondering when you'll notice that floating upward movement, movement which, incidentally, has already begun to move up your arm. "

__Step 3__: We do another short pause. And during this brief pause, the subject's attention focuses on his left arm. The person is curious to see what will happen. **Very important!** *At this point, we must be very attentive to any small movement of the arm! As you move, you have to point this out to the person, "See, feel? They have already started movements "and say that the movement increases. Remember that you must try to associate the feelings of the subject to your words, so that it is easier to get suggestions and orders cause sensory or motor responses. As you move your arm, tell him now concentrate on feel like your arm starts to go up and up ... That's fine, right, you're doing great ... continua well.*

__**IMPORTANT**__ This is the first suggestion (covert order) to be answered by the subject. (Keep in mind that there are some people who react quickly in the first 45 seconds or 2 minutes, others on the contrary take longer, because of this, while the subject begins not raise his left arm, do not continue with this technique, continues to subliminal suggestions as those who have been given in the last two 3 steps. If you see that you take 3 minutes (you have to have patience) and no movement, it is advisable that you ask the subject to relax and breathe deeply, and I invite you voluntarily move his left arm a little. you say this will help begin the movements of levitation and motivate to that will give you the boost you need. If after another 3 minutes the person does not react as would drink have responded, quiet okay, maybe that's not the best time to hypnotize him, maybe another day. (But if the tests answered correctly, it has been very responsive and already has levitating arm and elevation climbed a distance learner considered ... So, that means that everything is going great). Once respond and go high arm and has kept levitating a few seconds we continue with the following steps ...

__step 4__ "As long as your arm starts to rise and levitate, you will realize that the feeling is pleasant and relaxes more and more ... Now allow yourself to feel your left arm is becoming lighter and lighter, light as a feather, I light as the wind, light as balloons flying more and more "

Give suggestions and levitation associate any movement has occurred, because his left arm is completely relaxed, completely light and begins to levitate and rise. (When speaking, try to make your words sound light (as if you spoke slowly and calmly) Continue to give suggestions (covert orders) of this type until the left arm starts to rise completely Then apprentice; ... To reach this point, you continue:

step 5 *"Now I want you to notice as the left arm rises, rises and begins to climb higher and higher ... That's right, right, well, keep it up. Allow yourself to begin to realize that you feel a strange sense of lightness your left arm, while the whole hand is raised as if to fly free in the air, like a feather, as if your left arm was tied to a bunch of balloons multicolored rising to the heights of heaven. It feels like your left arm goes up, up, higher and higher, higher and higher, how light you feel your arm, so light that makes you easy to feel levitate and more and more! "That's perfect, you do very well ... Give suggestions of the same type until the left arm lift ... When the arm is raised and say to him: Now "Notice how your left arm is raised up, up, up, high, slightly above. That's right, well, now higher, a little higher ... higher ... higher ... "well you've done it ...*

If we succeed, and the person raises his arm, then we reached our goal and we end the year ...

END OF THE YEAR ...

IMPORTANT POINT: As we have previously studied before, we learned that this technique of suggestion and hypnotic induction levitation Arm Test (Family Sensory) is; Hypnotic either a downrigger states and is also a disguised test according to the purpose we want to achieve at any given time.

If we are to continue the exercise and use it as some downrigger United hypnotics; then, to find that the person responded well to the first 5 steps, and is fully raised hand, and that is deeply relaxed state Z1, then we could continue with two more steps ... In this case it would be Step 6 and Step 7; and would continue as follows, to deepen the hypnotic state and introduce more fully in the Z2 state.

Remember; do not pass here while the arm is not raised ... :-)

In the following paragraphs, in steps 6 and 7 when we say a phrase, such as: has the words: relaxed and calm. We have to say that phrase as if our words were relaxed and calm.

Same with the word "dream" have to say that phrase as if you really dream you had. But, you say what you say, or whatever you do (Never and never yawn!). And it will be easier to assimilate by the unconscious SLEEPING order; and induce deep sleep state you are suggesting through the suggestions (covert orders) and finally pronouncing the word dream and go to sleep, the person into a state of deep hypnotic trance.

Arm Levitation Test (Family Sensorial) downrigger United hypnotics

step 6 Now I want you to feel like your left arm (you have contact) rises and goes straight to your face slowly and touch your face ... The other arm remains stationary, but the left arm (you have contact) rises higher and higher towards your face until finally touches your face ... that is, you're doing very well.

step 7 Now notice how your left arm (contact you) begins to levitate and float up toward your face and gently touches your face. That's right, once as and your hand is near your face and subtly caressing your face (you touch, touches his hand with a finger and Draw it gently to your face insinuating that hand and began stroking his face, always subtle and always keeping the suggestion that now you order and tell). Now allow yourself to feel as you gently feel the sensation in your face fingers of your hands gently caress your face, comes more and more into a deep hypnotic trance state ... (Here you approach the person and begin to rock her, moving slightly from side to the other, or back and forth, to stimulate the feeling of deep relaxation and generate the "State of Trance Hypnotic Desire) and you order saying Now, you walk into a deep sleep, sleep more and more deeply, you slip deeper and deeper into a deep hypnotic sleep ... Now when I count to three you will relax even more, and you will sleep deeper and deeper still. 1 lose yourself relax 2, 3 sleep feels, now sleep!*

END WE DID IT AGAIN ...
XD apprentice, we have reached the end of this interesting chapter ^ _ ^

Good **LEARNERS**, This **It has been everything in this 2 BOOK SERIES: Applied NLP, Influence, Persuasion, suggestion and hypnosis** - Volume March 2! we have reached the end of our hypnosis course Practice ... wuao how time passes and as we advance quite right? Well, he apprenticed as it has always been a pleasure being with you in this journey to your excellent staff, on its way to become the hypnotist GREAT UNTIL NOW HAS TO BE ACHIEVED. Remember that if you feel any questions or there are some things we've learned that you LOVE clarify more *(You know you can always count on me for anything; I'm your mentor and great friend ")* ...

If there is something that may not yet fully understand or master; as I always say, take it easy, you're right, just calm apprentice and keep trying again and again, and you'll see how you managed to conquer and achieve everything you set your mind ...^ _ ^. Always keep in mind that all discipline is learned precept by precept and line upon line. As you take action, and implementing these teachings is to that extent that angers assimilating each principle, and as you assimilate each principle, these increasingly part of you will be ... until poufs you perform naturally like the greatest hypnotists and hypnotists in the world ... and this apprentice; is the most wonderful thing you can experience at the time, when you see what you've accomplished, thanks to your good positive mental attitude, your dedication, patience, persistence and perseverance ... Well apprentice, remember that *"If you have any questions, you can post it on my Website "or" email me directly to my mail (E-mail) "*.

MásterCoach.YlichTarazona@gmail.com
http://www.reingenieriamentalconpnl.com

If you enjoyed this workshop hypnosis, and want to "help" with your contribution, to support me to continue doing this wonderful work, which, with love, prepared for you. You can do this through the following link or Link.

Paypal@Donación.com
Thank you for your contribution

THE ROAD TO EXCELLENCE "Alone; When you think big, when you think you can, when you have the conviction and certainty that you will achieve and you determine out of your comfort zone. And you start to persevere in your vision and mission of purpose, to achieve reach each and every one of your most cherished goals and put your plans into action firmly to go after your dreams and start believing in yourself. So is there; you started will enjoy the results have conquered your goals proposed before. "- YLICH TARAZONA. -

APPRENTICE Remember that if you have not read my first book in the series: Applied NLP, Influence, Persuasion, suggestion and hypnosis - Volume 1 of 3 "*THE POWER OF HYPNOSIS*" *(Theoretical and Practical Manual Training HYPNOSIS and Skills Development Hypnotic Persuasive)*, You can get it on this **link.**

Or if you've already read both Volume 1, like this one, which is Volume 2 ... Then APPRENTICE invites you to read the last of the trilogy. "*HYPNOSIS TO THE NEXT LEVEL*". ***(Mastering the Art of Advanced hypnotism, self-hypnosis, regressions and hypnotic phenomena of the higher levels of Unconscious)***.

FINAL WORDS

Good champions and champions "{(CONGRATULATIONS)}" because we have reached the end of this wonderful hypnosis course practice in its special edition, with such dedication that I wrote for you. It was a long process of training and learning together you and I rode on this journey to your success and personal fulfillment.

This book will create and design thinking of you as a systematically INSTRUCTION MANUAL HANDY step; in order to go passing you by a mental process of continuous training learning through a "{(action pattern)}" well prepared and simplified to grant effective, optimal, effective, permanent results by the most powerful tools and methodologies of modern hypnosis, trance and phenomena hypnotics, suggestions and inductions High Level Testing Suggestibility, Covert Testing, Convincing and Downriggers combined hypnotic states with the most advanced techniques and methodologies HYPNOSIS psycholinguistics and APPLIED (NLP).

Remember APPRENTICE, if you really want to deepen in this masterful art of hypnosis and hypnotism to higher levels ... invite you to read the full TRILOGY SERIES: PNL Applied Influence, Persuasion, suggestion and hypnosis - Volume 1, 2 and 3.

YOU IMAGINE all you can achieve getting to learn to master these hypnosis techniques correctly. You can imagine how your life would change dramatically for the better, to be able to conquer all your dreams and goals you set out to achieve with hypnosis, thanks to these principles. NOW POSSIBLE!

Remember, take action and
MAKE THINGS HAPPEN
And start living a wonderful life
Principles centered, with the highest standards of integrity and uprightness
And I promise that if you live these Rules
You and I soon see us in the
CUSP OF EXCELLENCE

Your great friend COACH YLICH TARAZONA

ABOUT THE AUTHOR

PROFESSIONAL BACKGROUND:

Transformational Coach YLICH TARAZONA: Renowned writer, best-selling author, speaker and lecturer International High Level.

Expert in NLP or Neuro Linguistic Programming, Reengineering Brain, bioprogramming Mental, Neuro Coaching, Persuasion and Hypnosis.

Considered in various media as one of the most prominent and influential within the field of neuroscience and personal excellence MOTIVATIONAL Entrepreneurs; destined to have a legacy in the lives of thousands of people, through their passion, enthusiasm, dynamism and principle-centered leadership.

Man, of faith and Christian convictions; centered Principles and Values.

Reengineering founder MENTAL portal PNL ®- Virtual Community for Entrepreneurs. One of the Internet Website dedicated to providing COACHING in consolidating Skills and Development of Human Potential Maximum. Specialists in training, education and training of high level through neurolinguistics programming.

Creator PERSONAL COACHING SYSTEM Reengineering and bioprogramming MENTAL CEREBRAL to achieve goals, to define objectives and develop effective results optimal performance; through a series of audios, Podcasters, Tele-Seminars Online, Audio-Visual Workshops, Webinars and Conferences Master of attending classes.

Co-Creator and Re-designer of "NLP model" and effective formula "{(E - SMART - ER)}" [for the establishment and goal setting, action plan and principles of strategic planning to achieve and consolidate objectives].

Webminars creator Audio Visual, teleseminar Online and KEYNOTE [Re-Discovering Your Life Purpose and Mission].

Recognized "Author of the book series, sequences and EBOOK'S KEYNOTE" of [Reengineering CEREBRAL and bioprogramming MENTAL © -®]. Among the highlights we "As Improving Your Self-Esteem", "Liberate the Internal Self-Sabotage", "Rediséñate and Reinvent Your Life Position your personal brand or Personal Branding, Reengineering thought processes among others.

Best-selling author series [THE MASTERS OF CYCLES duplication and multiplication in the MARKETING NETWORKS Law and Universal Principles to Develop Your Business Multilevel professionally] Vol. 1, 2 and 3.

Creator of INTEGRAL SYSTEM PERSONAL COACHING through NLP or Neuro Linguistic Programming to produce positive changes in thought patterns, and generate effective results of high performance and optimal performance, both individual and organizational levels. Said TRAINING SYSTEM Offline and Online have marked the lives of hundreds of entrepreneurs in person and has changed the mental paradigms of thousands of people worldwide virtual path. Inspire participants, they hear, see or read his teachings; to live extraordinarily focused on principles.

PURPOSE AND PERSONAL VISION MISSION:

MY PURPOSE: Convey to all my readers faith; and the strength to move forward, always with confidence and optimism despite adversity. Guiding them as his mentor and coach staff find their life mission through a real opportunity for personal growth, to help them clarify their ideas, set goals, and develop a well-defined plan of action, enabling them to successfully conquer your wildest dreams. Allowing them to create their own future, writing the story of his own life and forging their own destiny through a continuous cycle of tactics and strategies created for that purpose.

Similarly, I want to help my readers, trainees, participants and supporters to change negative thought patterns and limiting mindsets, teaching them to consolidate their skills and develop their maximum human potential.

MY MISSION: Becoming an instrument in God's hands, that allows me to impact the lives of hundreds, thousands and millions of people around the world.

Leave a mark that makes a difference in the lives of the people I teach and carry my message. And also leave them a legacy that transcends time. And let them evolve in all transcendental and important aspects of their lives, both personally, spiritually, emotionally as well as professionally, academically and financially.

MY VISION: Bringing people hope and an option that allows them to transform their lives for the better, to help them develop that seed of greatness we all carry within its interior, and encourage them to consolidate position and expand their maximum human potential, next level of success.

And finally, to establish a connection and empathy with all my readers, participants and supporters, to let me go climbing in the relationship with each of them, as far as possible. At the same time, I teach them to position and consolidate in all aspects of life in a balanced way ...

Helping them internalize the correct principles that allow them to reinvent itself, creating a new and improved version of themselves. Opening up new paths, new opportunities aperturandoles success, enabling them to lead their lives, to find himself on the road to transformation and personal excellence. And finally; resume more strongly, his path to success and personal excellence ...

OTHER PUBLICATIONS, SPECIAL EDITIONS, MINI COURSES, BOOKS BY THE AUTHOR

Hello such, my great friend and friend reader, was a pleasure to have shared with you this time reading, I hope you enjoyed the most of the information in this book so lovingly prepared for you.

If you want to know some other of my works on Kindle from Amazon and CreateSpace I invite you to visit the following links. you great friend goodbye Coach YLICH TARAZONA

1.- *HOW TO IMPROVE YOUR SELF-ESTEEM. Learn to program your mind and focus your thoughts to conquer everything that you propose in Life.*
Amazon Kindle https://www.amazon.com/dp/B071NS4NPH
Paperback CreateSpace https://www.createspace.com/6763814

2.- *Liberate the self-sabotaging. Learn to Strengthen Your Inner Warrior, Energy Balance your channels, control your emotions and direct your thoughts.*
Amazon Kindle https://www.amazon.com/dp/B0716BWKR1
Paperback CreateSpace https://www.createspace.com/7120751

3.- *REDISÉÑATE and re YOUR LIFE. The Art REDESIGN your life, REINVENT, BE REBORN and create a new and improved version of yourself.*
Amazon Kindle https://www.amazon.com/dp/B06XKCSTNZ
Paperback CreateSpace https://www.createspace.com/7195297

4.- *REDISCOVERING your life purpose. Foundations for Living a Full Life, principle-centered and connected with Our Vision and Mission.*
Amazon Kindle https://www.amazon.com/dp/B071FFVVM4
Paperback CreateSpace https://www.createspace.com/7195692

5.- *THE POWER OF GOALS. Principles of Strategic Planning to achieve and consolidate your dreams and goals step by step.*
Amazon Kindle https://www.amazon.com/dp/B071SF2QX7
Paperback CreateSpace https://www.createspace.com/6684686

6.- *POSITIONING YOUR BRAND PERSON. Consolidate and establish your PERSONAL BRANDING in a competitive market through the "Love Brand".*
Amazon Kindle https://www.createspace.com/6799772
Paperback CreateSpace https://www.createspace.com/6615804

7.- *NEURO-LINGUISTIC PROGRAMMING. Practical Guide PNL COMPLETED - Modern Methodologies and Techniques for Effective Change Your Life*.
Kindle Amazon https://www.amazon.com/dp/B072DVXBHR
Paperback CreateSpace https://www.createspace.com/7119256

8.- *The power of metaphors and figurative language. Stories, parables, metaphors and allegories, Powerful Persuasive Communication Tools*.
Amazon Kindle https://www.amazon.com/dp/B01ESBD7WY
Paperback CreateSpace https://www.createspace.com/6685297

9.- *Reengineering CEREBRAL AND REDESIGN OF THOUGHT. Learn to reprogram Your Mental Processes and generate a Personal Reinvention*.
Amazon Kindle https://www.amazon.com/dp/B0723BVN9G
Paperback CreateSpace https://www.createspace.com/6685293

10-. *THE POWER OF HYPNOSIS. Theoretical and Practical Manual Training HYPNOSIS and Skills Development Hypnotic Persuasive*.
Amazon Kindle https://www.amazon.com/dp/B076G97F14
Paperback CreateSpace https://www.createspace.com/7691037

eleven-. *PRACTICAL COURSE OF HYPNOSIS. How to hypnotize, anyone, Anytime, Anywhere*.
Amazon Kindle https://www.amazon.com/dp/B076G97F14
Paperback CreateSpace https://www.createspace.com/7691037

12-. *HYPNOSIS TO THE NEXT LEVEL. Advanced hypnotism, self-hypnosis, regression and Hypnotic Phenomena High Level*.
Amazon Kindle https://www.amazon.com/dp/B076G97F14
Paperback CreateSpace https://www.createspace.com/7691037
Coming soon...

13-. *THE BIG BOOK OF HYPNOSIS. Hypnotism manual to learn hypnotize Anyone, Anytime, Anywhere*.
Amazon Kindle https://www.amazon.com/dp/B076G97F14
Paperback CreateSpace https://www.createspace.com/7691037
Coming soon...

14.- *Multilevel marketing networks. Masters Cycles of duplication and multiplication in the Network Marketing*.
Amazon Kindle https://www.amazon.com/dp/B01IZTHD0M
Paperback CreateSpace https://www.createspace.com/6614144

15.- *PLANNING BUSINESS NOTEBOOK. Monthly Action Plan to Develop Your Business Successfully Multilevel professionally*.
Amazon Kindle https://www.amazon.com/dp/B01J1JEVHI
Paperback CreateSpace https://www.createspace.com/6612779

16.- *NETWORK MARKETING TO THE NEXT LEVEL. Universal principles to develop your MLM Project Successfully professionally*.
Amazon Kindle https://www.amazon.com/dp/B01MFDJNT9
Paperback CreateSpace https://www.createspace.com/6619923

17.- *MULTILEVEL MARKETING NETWORK. Network Marketing Business Opportunity Great XXI Century, Towards your financial freedom*.
Amazon Kindle https://www.amazon.com/dp/B01M5H4CG2
Paperback CreateSpace https://www.createspace.com/6669735

18. *WORDS AND PHRASES FAMOUS INSPIRATIONAL. Collection with more than 800 Thoughts and motivational quotes Leaders Largest in History*.
Amazon Kindle https://www.amazon.com/dp/B01J4MGSU0
Paperback CreateSpace https://www.createspace.com/6615169

19.- *PNL applied to communication. Patterns Persuasion, Conversational Hypnosis and Hypnotic Oratory, the Art of Persuasion, and Influence Others Positively*.
Amazon Kindle https://www.amazon.com/dp/B01MXT273E
Paperback CreateSpace https://www.createspace.com/6762851
Coming soon...

20.- *THE ART OF COACHING WITH NLP. Knowledge, Skills, Techniques, Coaching Practices and Strategies to achieve goals and achieve what thou meanest in the Living*.
Amazon Kindle https://www.amazon.com/dp/B01N1N49V8
Paperback CreateSpace https://www.createspace.com/6762787
Coming soon...

21.- *Reengineering MENTAL CEREBRAL and programming. A quantum leap in the evolution of SER - The New Era of Thought and The Awakening of Consciousness*.
Amazon Kindle https://www.amazon.com/dp/B01EQML2U4
Paperback CreateSpace https://tsw.createspace.com/6685305
Coming soon...

22.- *LAW AND UNIVERSAL PRINCIPLES OF SUCCESS.* **Biblical Principles for Success and Abundance Living in accordance with the Lord's Way**.
Amazon Kindle https://www.amazon.com/dp/B01MQQWLGT
Softcover CreateSpace https://www.createspace.com/6762826
Coming soon...

To acquire other PRESENTATION OPTIONS and I acquired the BOOKS in versions STANDARD SOFT COVER or PREMIUM, PROFESSIONAL HARD COVER WITH or WITHOUT COVER, WITH or WITHOUT BACK COVER, in different qualities of prints (Black and White, Full Color, Premium Bonded Sheet) in Size Pocket, American Printing or Spiral ...

You can make them through my other OFFICIAL Portals.

http://www.lulu.com/spotlight/Coach_YlichTarazona
http://www.autoreseditores.com/coach.ylich.tarazona

Constant learning, continuous training and ongoing study are the keys among those who achieve success, those who do not. - Ylich Tarazona. -

PUBLICATIONS, EDITIONS, BOOKS, AND SPECIAL REPORTS CREATED BY THE AUTHOR

OTHER PUBLICATIONS, EDITIONS, BOOKS, AND SPECIAL REPORTS CREATED BY THE AUTHOR

CONTINUATION OF THE SERIES

WORKSHOPS, CONFERENCES, SEMINARS, MINI COURSES CREATED BY THE AUTHOR

AUDIO BOOKS, PODCASTS, WEBINARS, AND VIDEOS CREATED BY THE AUTHOR

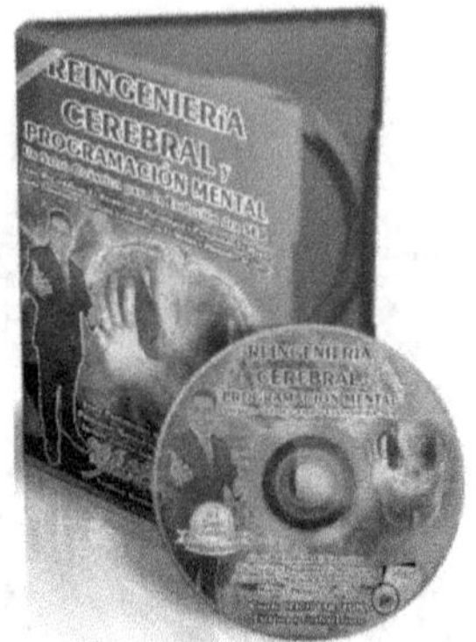

FOLLOW US THROUGH ALL OUR SOCIAL NETWORKS (SOCIAL MEDIA AND OFFICIAL WEBSITE)

Facebook, Twitter, YouTube, Google +, BlogSpot, Instagram, Pinterest, SlideShare, Speaker, LinkedIn, Skype y Gmail

https://www.amazon.com/Ylich-Eduard-Tarazona-Gil/e/B01INP4SU6
http://www.reingenieriamentalconpnl.com/
http://www.coachylichtarazona.com/

http://www.lulu.com/spotlight/Coach_YlichTarazona

http://www.autoreseditores.com/coach.ylich.tarazona

https://www.facebook.com/coachmaster.ylichtarazona

https://www.youtube.com/user/coachylichtarazona

https://plus.google.com/+ylichtarazona/posts

http://www.spreaker.com/user/ylich_tarazona

http://instagram.com/coach_ylich_tarazona/

https://www.pinterest.com/ylich_tarazona/

https://www.linkedin.com/in/ylichtarazona

http://es.slideshare.net/ylichtarazona

https://twitter.com/ylichtarazona

You can also contact the AUTHOR directly via e-mail by:
MasterCoach.YlichTarazona@gmail.com

Skype: Coaching_Empresarial

3rd Special Edition Revised and updated by: Ylich Tarazona November 2017.
Cover Design and development by: Ylich Tarazona
SEAL*: Independently Published* © /Kindle eBook **ASIN: B076G97F14**

ISBN-13: 978-1979723954

ISBN-10: 1979723958

BISAC: Hypnotism / Hypnosis / Self Hypnosis / Hypnotherapy / Hypnosis
YLICH TARAZONA the right to be identified as the author of this work has been affirmed by SafeCreative.org, Registration Code: 1710134545955 accordance with the Copyright Worldwide. **Publication Date:** *November 18, 2017.*

www.ingramcontent.com/pod-product-compliance
Lightning Source LLC
Chambersburg PA
CBHW050917260726

48660CB00001B/252